Treasures of the
Ashmolean Museum

PRÆMIA
HONORARIA.

EX UNO OMNIA

Treasures of the Ashmolean Museum

An illustrated souvenir
of the collections

David Piper

with additional entries
by
Christopher White

Ashmolean Museum · Oxford
1995

First produced for the Ashmolean Museum by Pevensey Press in association with Book Production Consultants, Cambridge and published in 1985, with sponsorship from Barclays Bank Plc.

Typeset in Baskerville by Westholme Graphics Ltd., and printed in Hong Kong. Reprinted 1990. Original ISBN:
Paperback 0 907849 09 1   Hardback 0 907849 99 7

Revised edition published 1995
ISBN 1 85444 059 4 paperback
ISBN 1 85444 060 8 hardback

Front cover: Detail from Uccello's *Hunt in the Forest* (Plate 49)

Back cover: Statuette of the Egyptian God Ptah (Plate 118)

Frontispiece: Elias Ashmole (1617–92) by John Riley, *c.* 1681, canvas, 124 × 101 cm. The Founder of the Ashmolean Museum. This portrait was probably painted for presentation with his gift of his collection to the University (see Introduction). The frame was carved for him by Grinling Gibbons.

Photographs throughout produced by the Museum's Photographic Department, with the exception of 103 (Victoria and Albert Museum) and 24 (a) – (g) (R.L. Wilkins, F.S.A.).

Printed and bound in Hong Kong 1995

Introduction

On 21 May 1683 the Duke of York (later King James II) and his Duchess, accompanied by the Lady Anne (later Queen Anne), inaugurated the freshly installed Ashmolean Museum on Broad Street in its newly completed building next to the Sheldonian Theatre. They inspected the 'rareties', partook of a sumptuous banquet, and then were shown (downstairs in the 'Elaboratory') 'some experiments to their great satisfaction'. Three days later, on 24 May, there was an open day for all doctors and masters of the University; some came, some did not. Some, according to Anthony Wood, antiquarian and historian of the University, were delighted. Others were not ('baubles'). From Christ Church, according again to Anthony Wood, there came no one at all.

The foundation was not greeted with undue reverence in all quarters. Oxford does not always welcome the new with enthusiasm, even when, as in the nature of museums, the new includes rich representation of the old. Since 1683, the fortunes of the Ashmolean have waxed and waned and waxed again. The founding collections, which Elias Ashmole (*frontispiece*) had promised by gift to the University of Oxford in 1677, and which were supplemented in his bequest of 1692, consisted predominantly of those 'rareties' that the royal gardeners, the Tradescants, John I and John II (*overleaf*) had accumulated in the first half of the seventeenth century. For that collection, Ashmole and Dr Wharton had compiled the first museum catalogue to appear in Britain, the *Musaeum Tradescantium*, published in 1656. In 1659, three years before his death, John Tradescant II made the collection over to Ashmole by deed of gift. The former, with no surviving male heir, had been concerned, but uncertain, about the future of the family collections; one of his ideas had been that it might go to Oxford or Cambridge. Ashmole had become a member of Brasenose while in Oxford during the Civil War, and it was to Oxford that the collections came.

Ashmole's views as to the role that his museum should play are recorded in some detail, though not all his ideas were to be realised. His Tradescant catalogue records a collection that may seem entirely in the tradition of the old 'Wunderkämmer', those miscellanies of 'rareties' that princes and some learned men all over Europe were prone to accumulate during the sixteenth and early seventeenth centuries – the spoil of voyages over an expanding globe no less than of human ingenuity and art; exotic natural curiosities, freaks, relics. It includes a dodo, shells, precious stones, weapons, shoes, Chinese lanterns, red Indian hunting shirts, fish, coins and medals. Yet the catalogue is set out according to a scheme of classification; even if rudimentary, it does herald those processes of intellectual and scientific ordering that were to lead to the catalogues of modern museums, to storage of information in computers.

Later on, when Ashmole was brooding on the ways in which he would expect his museum to be developed by his University and drafted its 'Statutes, Orders and Rules' (1686), his concerns were very much in key with those of that new body of scientists, the Royal Society, of which he was indeed a very early member. C.H. Josten has noted his 'zeal for the promotion of the natural sciences . . . also his appreciation of the importance of factual, as opposed to speculative, research'. He insisted on the need for 'the inspection of Particulars, especially those as are extraordinary in their Fabrick, or usefull in Medicine, or applyed to Manufacture or Trade'. This last concern, for the service a museum might offer to 'Manufacture or Trade', almost anticipates the aims of the South Kensington Museum following on the didactic and improving aims of Albert, Prince Consort.

In fact, the 'elaboratory' in the lowest floor of the Ashmolean, where the Duke of York had viewed 'experiments' with such satisfaction, was to be the focus for much of the study of natural sciences in Oxford throughout the eighteenth century and beyond. The collections, however, declined rather than flourished. Ashmole had been aware of conservation problems, of the inevitable decay of organic specimens, but his stipulation that if a specimen had to be destroyed, a drawing should always be made of it first, was unfortunately not acted upon. A very great deal was lost, the most celebrated item being the remains of that bird described in the 1656 catalogue as 'Dodar, from the Island *Mauritius*; it is not able to flie being so big' – diagnosed as noisome and condemned, though its dessicated beak and other fragments still survive, now in the University Museum.

Nevertheless, the Ashmolean as Museum was far from forgotten. The standards of its curatorial practice may have been recorded by various visitors as (to

put it mildly) unsatisfactory, but when that great enterprise of European enlightenment, the *Encyclopédie*, focused on the subject of museums, the Ashmolean was the only one to be mentioned by name. Though not the first museum in the world to open to the public – the Tradescants, for example, in their house at Lambeth, seem to have opened to all enquirers – the Ashmolean was surely the first institutional museum to open to the public in Britain and survive, ante-dating the founding of the British Museum by seventy years. In the second quarter of the nineteenth century, after a period of some neglect of the collections, regeneration began.

Ashmole's original intentions, as far as the Natural Sciences were concerned, and the residue of the founding collections that illustrated them, were transplanted to the new University Museum (1855–60) and the ethnographical Pitt Rivers Museum (1885). About these, adjacent to the Parks, there was to grow up through the next century one of the major concentrations of scientific research in Europe; though now known as the 'Science Area', it might be as legitimately entitled 'Ashmolean' as is the Ashmolean Museum of today.

These dispersals were symptomatic of a gradual nineteenth century rationalisation in the development of academic disciplines in general. The present-day basic organisation of the Ashmolean Museum is due to the most remarkable of all the Keepers in its long history, Sir Arthur Evans (in office between 1884 and 1908), and his aider and abetter, one of the most determined of all benefactors, Mr C.D.E. Fortnum (1820–99). They were virtually the second (joint) Founders of the Museum, and responsible for its move from its original home on Broad Street (now, aptly, the Museum of the History of Science) to C.R. Cockerell's superb neo-Grecian building (1845) on Beaumont Street, designed to house the University Galleries and the University's ancient marbles, and the Taylor Institution (for Modern Languages). The Galleries, previously in the Bodleian Library premises, date from 1623, and had formed the first art gallery available to the public; but their great importance accrued from 1846, when the University accepted from the Earl of Eldon and other subscribers a large part of the most remarkable collection of drawings by Raphael, Michelangelo and other masters that had belonged to Sir Thomas Lawrence (**57**, **58**). There followed further acquisitions of dazzling merit, including the Fox-Strangways gift (1850) of 40 early Italian paintings, among them Uccello's masterpiece *The hunt* (**49**); the prints and drawings from Francis Douce's bequest (1834) to the Bodleian (**59**); the Penrose bequest; the Chambers Hall gift of 1855; and, in 1881, John Ruskin's deposit of 36 watercolours by J.M.W. Turner.

The major holding of classical marbles consisted of the important remnants (**23**) of the great pioneering collection formed by the Earl of Arundel in the early seventeenth century, which had come gradually to the University through various benefactors. There were also the important inscriptions given by the great jurist John Selden (d. 1654) and other benefactors. The Bodleian Library itself held an accumulation of objects of historic and associated interest, other than books, some dating from well before the foundation of the Ashmolean – the most famous being Guy Fawkes's lantern (*below*), now a prime focus for the attention of children in the Ashmolean. From the 1850s the Ashmolean itself had accumulated more and more archaeological holdings of other than Greco-Roman interest: Anglo-Saxon and, more importantly, Egyptian material from a dedicated promoter of the Museum's progress, G.J. Chester. Pressure from him, and the formidable Fortnum and Evans, led ultimately to the consolidation of all these collections at Beaumont Street, where at last, in 1908, a statute pronounced them to constitute *The Ashmolean Museum of Art and Archaelogy*. This resolved into two Departments, Fine Arts and Antiquities, each with its Keeper. These were supplemented first by the Heberden Coin Room, extrapolated from Antiquities and fortified in 1921 by the transfer of the University coin collection (including Ashmole's) from the Bodleian Library (it now also houses the coin collections built up by many of the Colleges). The establishment of the Coin Room was aided by a benefaction from C.B. Heberden (like Ashmole, a Brasenose man). The Department of Eastern Art was opened in 1961; it brought together the University's oriental collections, mainly formerly in the Department of Fine Art (henceforward, of Western Art) and the old Indian Institute. A fifth Department, of a major collection of casts from antique sculpture, is curated, since the foundation of the Chair in 1884, by the Lincoln Professor of Classical Archaeology and Art. Since 1973 and the creation of a new post of overall Director, the Museum's administration has been highly centralised. Also incorporated in the Museum is the Griffith Institute for Egyptological Study.

From this brief history it can be seen that art, as such, has come under the Ashmolean Museum banner only since 1908; and the large number of illustrations in this book are from objects in the Department of Western Art may seem unjust. But *Treasures of the Ashmolean Museum* is designed as a souvenir for the visitor and not as a learned survey, and the majority of visitors are normally to be found in the Western Art galleries. Thus there is here only the merest glimpse of the contents of the Heberden Coin Room, in sheer quantity of items perhaps the largest Department of all but also, owing to its nature, the least visible to the non-specialist. There is little more than a glimpse of the richness and extraordinary range of Antiquities. That Department houses the surviving nucleus of the Tradescants' collection, including 'Powhatan's mantle' (*overleaf*); it is chiefly, however, the repository of a formidable representation of the early cultures of Europe, Egypt and the Near East, owing much to the Museum's close association and active involvement with field archaeology. Sir John Evans; his son, the great Keeper of the Ashmolean, Sir Arthur; Sir Flinders Petrie; Sir John Myres; Sir John Beazley – these are but a few of the

Opposite left John Tradescant the Elder *(d.1638), perhaps by Thomas or Emmanuel de Critz, canvas, 79 × 62 cm. Given by Elias Ashmole, 1683. Botanist, traveller, and founder of the Tradescant museum at Lambeth, John I was gardener to Charles I, the Duke of Buckingham, and other aristocrats. Appointed first Custodian at the Oxford Botanic Garden (opened 1621), he died before he could take up the post.*

Opposite right John Tradescant the Younger *(1608–62), perhaps by Thomas or Emmanuel de Critz, canvas, 107 × 86 cm. Given by Elias Ashmole, 1683. Very unusually and informally John II is shown as a working gardener, with a spade; he succeeded his father at Lambeth, and made over the collection by deed of gift to Ashmole.*

Left Guy Fawkes's lantern, *sheet iron, 34.5 cm high. Originally it had a horn window, and could also be closed completely to hide the light. Given to the University in 1641 by Robert Heywood, son of a Justice of the Peace who had been present at the arrest of Guy Fawkes in the cellars of Parliament House, when the 'Gunpowder Plot' was foiled on 5 November 1605. Transferred from the Bodleian Library to the Ashmolean in 1887.*

Opposite left 'Powhatan's mantle', *deerskin, with shell decoration, 235 × 160 cm. The most famous exhibit from the Tradescant Collection, which formed the major part of the Ashmolean's displays at its opening in 1683. A visitor to the Tradescant museum in 1638 recorded seeing there 'the robe of the King of Virginia' and it was later catalogued as 'Pohatan, King of Virginia's habit all embroidered with shells or Roanoke'. Powhatan was father of Princess Pocohontas. The 'mantle' may have had some function, such as a temple hanging, rather than being a garment.*

great benefactors of the Department. For the Heberden Coin Room, the Department of Antiquities, and no less for the Department of Eastern Art (enriched by spectacular benefactions), more specialised illustrative books could easily be compiled, and surely should be.

From Ashmole on, the role of benefactors to Oxford, benefitting all Departments, is formidable, and continues despite the factors weighing against such benefactions in the economic climate of the late twentieth century. The notes to the illustrations that follow can draw attention to only a few of the individual donors, but to all who have given, the Museum is most gratefully indebted. Recent purchases of importance have been aided repeatedly – as the notes record – by the National Art-Collections Fund, and more recently by the invaluable Friends of the Ashmolean (founded only in 1971), while the contributions from the National Exchequer via the Victoria and Albert Museum Purchase Grant Fund have been crucial for almost all major purchases over the last decade. The predecessor of this book, under the same title, was restricted to black and white reproductions. This replacement, in colour throughout, has been made possible by a very generous subvention from Barclays Bank – the University's bankers – whose decisive help it is a great pleasure to be able to record.

Above Human skull, *originally plastered and painted, from a Neolithic settlement at Jericho, c.7000 BC. One of several from the site, all with bivalve shells inset for eyes – perhaps one of the earliest attempts by man at portraiture. Given in 1955, from excavations in Jericho by Dame Kathleen Kenyon, it witnesses to the Museum's continuing close association with field archaeology.*

Left Flint handaxe, *12.5 cm long. From the collection of Sir John Evans (1823–1908), father of Sir Arthur Evans (who gave Sir John's collection in 1927) and a pioneer in Britain of scientific methods in prehistoric archaeology. It bears a characteristic John Evans label: acquired on his visit to France, 1859, to authenticate the discoveries of Boucher de Perthes, who had discovered stone artefacts in geological contexts.*

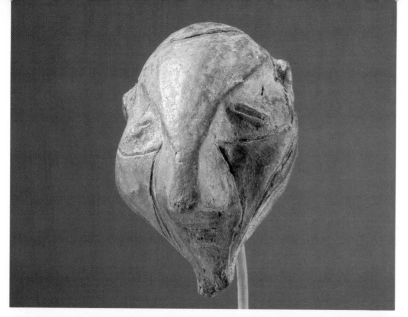

◄**1** Greek: *Statuette, head only*, terracotta, 5 cm high, *c.*4000 BC. From the site of Dikili Tash near Kavala, in Greek Thrace; it is in the tradition of Late Neolithic (Copper Age) plastic art. Acquired in 1920.

◄**2** Sardinian (Meragluc): *Statuette*, bronze, 77.5 cm high, of a shepherd carrying a sheep, characteristic in style and subject of the Meragluc culture of Sardinia, which flourished in the later second and early first millennia BC. Presented by Sir Arthur Evans in 1894, during his Keepership (bought in Cologne).

►3 Egyptian: *Ceremonial palette*,
slate, carved in low relief, 42.5 ×
22 cm, from Hierakonpolis,
temple, 'Main Deposit',
Protodynastic, *c.*3000 BC. One of a
collection of archaic objects
(including the 'Scorpion King'
macehead, also in the Ashmolean)
which had been put aside within
the temple area when no longer
needed later on. They display
many features which link them to
legendary accounts of the period
of transition from the prehistoric
Egypt of local chieftains to the
dynastic, united under one king
whose Upper Egyptian base may
have been in the area of
Hierakonpolis. Around the
reservoir for grinding eyepaint
snake the long necks of two
fabulous feline creatures whose
tongues lick a stumbling gazelle;
other gazelles below are pursued
by hounds wearing collars. On the
other side (not shown) is a mêlée of
combatant beasts, some fabulous,
some identifiable, and below them
a more peaceful, but enigmatic,
scene – a giraffe, a bull and a
gazelle prance to the music of a
jackal-headed flautist. Framing
the upper half are the elongated
bodies of two animals who appear
elsewhere in the scenes and have
been tentatively identified as
belonging to the dog family. The
hectic composition of the palette
suggests that it is an early member
of the small series to which it
belongs – the most famous being
the 'Narmer Palette' (Cairo), also
from Hierakonpolis, which shows
a more simple and orderly
decorative scheme. A Near
Eastern origin is often canvassed
for the portrayal of animals which
appear on other Protodynastic
material from this site, but not in
later Egyptian art. Given by the
Egyptian Research Account, 1908.

◄5 Egyptian: *Hedgehog vase*, pottery, red ware, 7.4 cm high, from tomb D 11 at Abydos, 18th Dynasty, reign of Tuthmosis III (*c*.1479–1425 BC). Polished, with decoration in relief, details painted in black. A somewhat abstract version of an animal usually treated with great realism in faience or pottery: a stylised tree forms arabesques over the creature's rump, and behind the spout is a tiny handle. Given by the Egypt Exploration Fund, 1908.

◄4 Egyptian: *Hippopotamus*, pottery, coarse red ware, 27.3 cm long, from grave 134 at Hu, Predynastic (*c.*3500–3000 BC). Hippopotami abounded in prehistoric Egypt, to judge by the many models that have survived. Associated by the ancient Egyptians with the deity Taweret, protectress of babies and mothers in childbirth, today they inhabit the river no further north than Khartoum. Given by the Egypt Exploration Fund.

►6 Egyptian: *A scribe and priest of the god Thoth*, limestone, 31.5 cm high, from Ashmunein (ancient Hermopolis), New Kingdom, 19th Dynasty (1307–1196 BC). The scribe wears a priestly leopard skin over his pleated linen tunic and carries on his shoulders a baboon, sacred animal of Thoth, the god of writing who serves as the gods' own scribe. The animal is rendered with a rather pleasing naturalness which relieves the formality of the statue; the line formed by its paws across the man's forehead and the fall of its shaggy upper coat around his ears mimic the contours of the wig which one would normally expect to see here – a typically neat Egyptian solution to the problem of depicting an unusual subject within the accepted artistic norms. In his right hand the man holds a softly folded object, perhaps a bag of writing equipment. Three columns of hieroglyphic inscription on the back of the statue invoke a funerary offering of Thoth for the scribe, who served in his temple at Hermopolis; his name is unfortunately lost with the lower part of the statue. Acquired in 1961, with the aid of the National Art-Collections Fund.

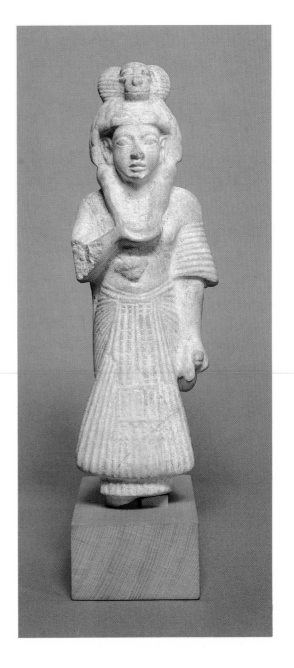

▲ **7** Syrian(?): *A cow and calf among papyrus plants*, ivory plaque, 12.6 × 6.6 cm, for inlay, *c*.850–700 BC. The piece of wooden furniture from which it comes was taken as booty or tribute to the Assyrian king in whose storehouse at Nimrud, in northern Iraq, it was found by modern excavators. A favourite theme of the period, symbolising fertility.

◄ **8** Iranian: *Humped-backed bull (zebu)*, pottery, 39 cm long, 26 cm high, from Gilan, north-west Iran, *c*.1350–1000 BC. The potters of prehistoric Iran (like the local metalworkers, also well represented in the Ashmolean) were particularly fond of animal designs, whether painted on pottery or in free-modelled vessels of this kind, which were placed in graves in considerable numbers in the Early Iron Age. When first discovered (1950s), they proved so attractive that numerous copies were made by modern potters. This one has been authenticated by a thermoluminescence test.

▼ **9** Egyptian: *The daughters of Akhenaten and Nefertiti* (The 'Princesses' Fresco), fresco, painted plaster, 40 × 165 cm, from Tell el-'Amarna (ancient Akhetaten), late 18th Dynasty, 1353–1335 BC. The fragmentary fresco is part of a domestic scene of the royal family which once decorated a private house, perhaps that of a loyal courtier, in the new capital city of the Pharaoh Akhenaten. Two bejewelled younger daughters, Neferure and Neferneferuaten, are perched on cushions at the feet of their mother, the red sash of whose dress falls obliquely behind them. Between her feet and those of their father, seated on a stool at the right, are the legs of the three elder daughters: the sixth, baby Setepenre, probably sat on her mother's lap. This is one of the many scenes of the private life of the royal family which are such a distinctive feature of the unorthodox art of the Amarna period – when Akhenaten, inspired by a new religious cult, a form of sun-worship, instigated a vivid (though short-lived), relatively naturalistic and more personal episode in the long history of the severely formal conventions of Egyptian art. Excavated by Flinders Petrie; other isolated fragments of the scene are in the Petrie Museum, University College, London, and the Manchester Museum. Given by W.M.F. Petrie and H. Martyn Kennard, 1893.

▼**10** Chinese: *Burial urn*, coil-made with red earthenware with red and black slip painted decoration, 48.3 cm high, *c*.3000 BC. It came probably from Banshan, Gansu, north-west China: the finest of such pots, like this, technically assured and confident, are amongst the most accomplished in the medium to be made by a Neolithic people anywhere. From the Sir Herbert Ingram gift, 1956.

►**11** Chinese: *Bronze vessel*, 19.7 cm high, tomb furniture, late Shang dynasty (11th century BC). Essentially, it is a cooking utensil miniaturised for ritual use; the type is known as *Li Ding*. The highly formalised decorations on the body are abstracted from images of two *Kui* dragons, while the design round the neck evokes cicadas that bury themselves in the earth to emerge as singing insects – symbols of the re-birth, obviously apt for burial ritual. From the Sir Herbert Ingram gift, 1956.

◄**12** Cretan: *Pithos with octopus design*, baked clay, 74.5 cm high, late Minoan period II (*c.*1450 BC). One of the most important groups of material in the Ashmolean is the Cretan collection, formed largely from the excavations at Knossos conducted by a former Keeper of the Museum, Sir Arthur Evans, between 1900 and 1906, and given to him by successive Cretan and Greek governments in recognition of his work. The most characteristic decorative motifs employed in Minoan Crete in the Late Bronze Age were sea-creatures and marine plants. This *pithos* (storage jar) from Knossos is decorated with a sinister but stately octopus and (in the top left part in this view) a *murex* shell, the source of the purple dye which was highly prized throughout antiquity. Presented by Sir Arthur Evans.

►**13** Cycladic: *Figurine* ('idol'), white marble, 32 cm high, from the Cycladic island of Amorgos, 'Early Cycladic' (*c.*3000–2000 BC). Many such figurines have been found in tombs on Amorgos, Naxos, Melos and other Cycladic islands of the Aegean. They are now frequently called 'idols', but their true original function is wholly unknown. The present-day vogue for Cycladic art owes much to the interest shown in primitive art by such 20th-century artists as Picasso and Brancusi. The existence of similar figurines in Early Bronze Age Anatolia, Crete and Egypt witnesses to the close contact of the inhabitants of the silver-rich Cyclades with other important centres in the eastern Mediterranean, and their role as pioneers of sea-borne trade.

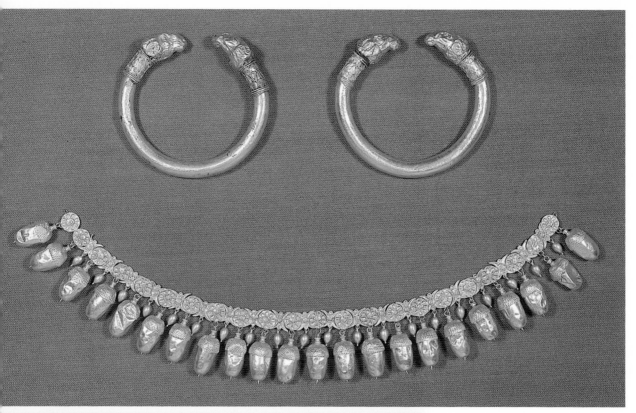

▲**14** Crimean (Scythian): *Necklace*, gold, 31 cm long, and *Bracelets*, gold on bronze, 8.5 cm diameter, from Grave IV at Nymphaeum in the Crimea (5th century BC). Acquired in 1885.

◄**15** Bulgarian (Scythian): *Mug and beaker*, silver, 9 cm and 11.5 cm. Found in a tomb of the late 5th century BC at Dalboki, Bulgaria, in 1879, and presented by the Seven Pillars of Wisdom Trust in memory of T.E. Lawrence in 1948.

▲ **16** Cypriot: *Barrel jug*, baked clay, 30 cm high, 7th–6th century BC. Bought in Larnaca, Cyprus, in 1885, this is an outstanding example of the Cypro-Archaic period. The elaborate combination of intricate geometric pattern with representational figure drawing, presented so boldly on an otherwise largely underworked surface, has come to be known as 'Free Field' style.

◄**17** Greek: *Vase (the 'Shoemaker' pelike)*, baked clay, 40 cm high, Attic black figure, attributed to the 'Eucharides painter', 5th century BC. Found in Rhodes. The Ashmolean has a strong showing of craftsmen at work, recorded on Greek vases. Beneath the table is a bowl of water with which the leather could be wetted before cutting. Above the shoemaker is a rack containing different kinds of knives used in his craft, accurately delineated. A customer is being fitted, and no doubt gossip is being exchanged.

►**18** Etruscan (Umbria): *Warrior*, bronze statuette, 28 cm high. Such figures attest to flourishing schools of bronze working in 5th-century Umbria. They illustrate a gradual stylisation, by local craftsmen, of classical Greek forms. This one obviously held a spear, threatening, in his hand.
Given by C.D.E. Fortnum.

▲ **19** Greek: *Cup*, baked clay, 12.8 cm diameter, Attic red figure, attributed to the Colmar Painter, *c*.500 BC. Found in Chiusi. Work and play combined: a boy carries a plate of food covered with a napkin in one hand, and trundles a hoop along with the other. This is a masterpiece of composition, designed to harmonise with the tondo form of the cup. Greek painting was a main source for the development of Western European art, but the large murals that once adorned great monuments have vanished. Some slight indication of the style and subject matter that informed them is offered by the very extensive survivals of Greek pottery. Many scholars have been involved in building up the impressively representative collection in the Ashmolean, not least Sir Arthur Evans, who gave this cup in 1886, but most famously Sir John Beazley (1885–1970), Lincoln Professor of Classical Archaeology and Art in Oxford, great analyst of the development of Greek painting and the styles of the individual painters, and benefactor of the Ashmolean.

►**20** Greek: *Silver stater*, 2 cm diameter (enlarged), Tarentum, *c*.380 BC. The reverse side, shown here, depicts Taras, the mythical founder of the city, riding the dolphin which, according to legend, his father the sea god Poseidon sent to his rescue when he was shipwrecked off the coast of Italy. The obverse shows a naked horseman armed with a shield, an allusion to the equestrian prowess of the Tarentines both on the field of battle and in the hippodrome. Gift of Sir Stanley Robinson, 1964.

►**21** Greek: *Ethiopian boy asleep*, baked clay, 6.3 cm high. From Tarentum (modern Taranto), and a miniature masterpiece of the Hellenistic modelling of the region. The boy, perhaps a slave, is curled up asleep at the base of a wine jar, perhaps exhausted, perhaps happily drunk. Given by Sir Arthur Evans, 1884.

◄**22** Greek: *Arsinoë*, gold octodrachm, 2.7 cm diameter (enlarged). Arsinoë was the wife of Ptolemy II, Philadelphus of Egypt (285–246 BC). Her deification, on her death in 270, diverted into the royal treasury a wealth of temple dues, of which this coin is one product. Its image of Arsinoë, shown veiled and wearing a stephane, is a particularly fine example of Hellenistic portraiture. The reverse side bears the name of Arsinoë and shows a double cornucopiae as a symbol of plenty.

►**23** Roman, from a Greek original: *Amazon*, marble, extant height 104 cm. A good Roman copy of a Greek 5th-century original. Pliny, the Roman encyclopaedist, tells the story of a competition in ancient Greece for a statue of an Amazon for the temple of Artemis at Ephesus. The artists involved (who included Phidias, Polyclitus, and Cresilas) had to choose the winner, and this proved to be the Amazon 'which each artist had placed second to his own', namely the one made by Polyclitus. The Ashmolean's Amazon may well relate to such a project. It is but one of the dozens of pieces of antique sculpture and inscriptions from the Arundel collection, formed in the early 17th century by Thomas Howard, Earl of Arundel (1585–1646), the pioneer collector in England of works of art from classical antiquity. They were kept at Arundel House, just south of the Strand, long since demolished. A first group came thence to Oxford at the instigation of John Evelyn (the diarist) in 1667; a further large group was given by Louisa, Dowager Countess of Pomfret, in 1757 (including this Amazon); a few other items followed at different times. Arundel's collection was assembled for him by agents active in Italy, Greece and the eastern Aegean. The nucleus preserved at Oxford, though very variable in quality, has considerable importance for the history of collecting in England and of taste.

a

b

24 *Engraved sealstones.* The use of seals as a means of authentification or identification, or simply decoration, goes back to at least the 7th millenium BC, and they constitute an invaluable repository of prehistoric and later imagery. Stamp seals and cylindrical ones were most usual in metal or stone, often semi-precious gems. The Ashmolean has a formidably rich representation from the eastern Aegean, Egypt and the Near Eastern regions, Greece and Italy. (*a*) Cretan (Knossos district): *Acrobats,* chalcedony, 1.8 × 2.1 cm, Middle Minoan period, 2nd millennium BC. Gift of Sir Arthur Evans, 1938. (*b*) Cretan (Palaikastro): *Dolphins,* flattened cylinder covered with hammered gold foil, 1.6 cm long, Middle Minoan period, 2nd millennium BC. Acquired 1938. (*c*) Greek (Trika, Thessaly): *Fox and grapes,* chalcedony, 1.6 × 2.1 cm, late 5th century BC. Bequeathed by G.J. Chester, 1892. (*d*) Etruscan (Tarquinia): *Scarab; a vulture threatens a coiled snake,* cornelian, 1.4 × 1 cm, late 5th century BC. (*e*) Greek: *Alexander the Great,* tourmaline (here photographed from an impression), 2.5 cm diameter, probably 4th century BC. A very early and very fine portrait of Alexander, perhaps made in an eastern area of his vast empire. Bought in Beirut and bequeathed by G.J. Chester, 1892. (*f*) Greek (Graeco-Persian): *Winged, horned lion,* chalcedony (here photographed from an impression), 2.7 × 2 cm, from Grave V at Nymphaeum, 5th or 4th century BC. An Achaemenid mythological beast, typical of Greek craftsmanship for Persian clients. (*g*) Greek: *'The Felix Gem',* cornelian, 2.6 × 3.5 cm, early 1st century, signed by the gem-cutter *Felix.* Diomedes and Ulysses escape from Troy with the *Palladium* (an image of Troy which the Greeks had to capture to be able to conquer Troy). It was made for a patron at the Roman imperial court: the Julio-Claudian dynasty derived its ancestry from exiles from Troy. A very famous gem, whose previous owners included Pope Paul II, the Earl of Arundel, Sir Arthur Evans and Captain E.G. Spencer-Churchill. Acquired with the aid of the Victoria and Albert Museum Purchase Grant Fund, 1966.

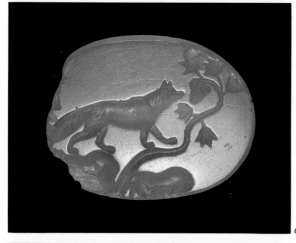

c

d

e

f

g

30

◄ 25 Egyptian: *Double-sided mummy portrait*, encaustic paint on wood, 38 × 14.8 cm, 4th century. The use of a painted portrait of the deceased to replace the impersonal mummy-mask of Egyptian tradition was a Graeco-Roman introduction: a relatively, but startlingly, naturalistic innovation. Likeness was clearly important, although the sitters are usually depicted in the prime of life, wearing their best clothes and jewellery, and there is evidence that some of the paintings at least may have hung on house walls before being adapted for funerary use. This example is unusual in being double-sided; its former owner, Sir John Beazley (who gave it in 1966), thought that the plain girl on the reverse side might be the elder sister of the pretty one on the front, but their close similarity suggests that they are the same girl: perhaps she was dissatisfied with the first, unflattering, version, and demanded a second, for which she changed her hairstyle. A remarkable number of these portraits have survived, preserved in the dry atmosphere of the Fayum area of northern Egypt; they date mostly from the first four centuries AD.

▲ 26 Roman: *Nero* (ruled 54–68), bronze sestertius, obverse, 3.6 cm diameter (enlarged). A fine example of the Roman genius for portraiture, combining an ideal view of imperial authority with a surely unflattering delineation of the individual features, and most skilfully finished. Although on a miniature scale, it conveys a most massive presence. Bequest of Sir Arthur Evans.

◄**27** Roman: *Lar*, bronze statuette, 21.5 cm high, 1st century. The deity of the home and family is shown dancing forward, his tunic awhirl with the vigour of his movements. With one hand he holds up an ibex-headed vessel (*rhyton*) from which he pours an offering into the dish (*patera*) held out in the other hand. On his head is a wreath of laurel or myrtle leaves. The eyes of the figurine are enhanced with silver, as are the fastenings at the shoulders and the boot buttons, and strips of silver let into the surface of the bronze indicate bands of purple colour in the tunic. This is the right-hand one of a pair which would have flanked a household altar, the *lavarium*. Many such altars, some complete with their figures, have been found at Pompeii, and there, also, the wall behind is often painted with a scene of a pair of Lares dancing attendance on a central figure – a Genius or a seated Vesta. The image of the dancing Lar became popular in the time of Augustus. Given by the Friends of the Ashmolean, 1971, and their first, most happy, gift to the Museum after their foundation.

▲ **28** Roman: *The Wint Hill bowl*, light greenish glass, 19 cm diameter, 5 cm deep, believed to have been made at Cologne, *c.* mid-4th century; found in 1956, in excavations at a Roman site at Wint Hill, Somerset. Engraved on the outside surface – a horseman and two hounds drive a hare into a net. Around the edge: VIVASCVMTVISPIES in Roman letters, comprising the Latin motto VIVAS CUM TVIS and the Greek πIE ZHCHC, meaning 'Long life to you; drink, and good health'. Presumably it was intended as a drinking vessel; the decoration links it to other examples with hunting, mythological and Christian scenes whose distribution is centred in the Rhineland. Purchased with the aid of the National Art-Collections Fund, 1957.

◄29 Anglo-Saxon: King Eadgar (959–75): *Silver penny*, minted in Oxford, 2.3 cm diameter (shown enlarged). The obverse (not shown) reads EADGAR REX ANG[L]OR̄V; the reverse MO[netarius] OXNA [ford] VRBIS. An early record both of the existence of Oxford as 'town', even 'city', and of the beginnings of its recurrent association with the minting of coinage.

▲30 Anglo-Saxon: *The Cuddesdon bowl*, brilliant blue glass with fine trailed decoration, probably Kentish, 11.5 cm diameter, *c*.600. The glass was found in a grave at Cuddesdon, Oxon., in 1847, with another (less complete), a bronze pail and jewelled bronze fittings from a harp – all the sort of accoutrements buried with Anglo-Saxons of noble rank. The princes of the West Saxons were fond of names beginning with the syllable Cuth (Cutha, Cuthred, Cuthwulf, etc.), and it is entirely possible that this grave was of a 'Cuth-person' who gave his name to the place, which over the years changed from 'Cuth's dun' (hill) to Cuddesdon. The bowl came to light during the building of a palace for the Bishop of Oxford, then William Wilberforce; it passed into his possession, and was eventually sold with the contents of his house and lost from view. It turned up again holding primroses on a mantlepiece in Northamptonshire and was there recognised by the keen eye of Miss Jocelyn Morris, curator at Warwick Museum. Purchased by the Museum in 1977 with the aid of grants from the National Art-Collections Fund, the Victoria and Albert Museum Purchase Grant Fund, and the Friends of the Ashmolean.

▲ **31** Anglo-Saxon: *The Alfred jewel*, gold, enamel, and rock crystal, 6.2 cm long, (max.) 3.1 cm wide, 1.3 cm deep. The gold frame bears the openwork inscription + *Aelfred mec heht gewyrcan* ('Alfred ordered me to be made'), suggesting strongly the association with King Alfred the Great (871–99). The seated figure holding the flowers is thought to represent sight, an allusion which corresponds with the function currently favoured for the jewel – that of terminal or handle for an *aestel* or pointer for following the text of a manuscript. Precious *aestels* were distributed by King Alfred with copies of his translation of Pope Gregory's *Pastoral care*. The jewel was found in 1693 at Newton Park, 4 miles south of Athelney, Somerset, an area associated with Alfred, and bequeathed by Nathaniel Palmer in 1718. It has long been amongst the handful of objects, if not *the* object, that most compels the fascination of visitors.

▶**33** Chinese: *Seated Bodhisattva*, fig-tree wood, over life-size, 13th century. In the Chinese Buddhist tradition, that still reflected Indian prototypes. Traces of painting (at two different periods) remain on a pink gesso ground. Originally it was probably in a cave temple in the Shanxi province; it came to Europe in the 1930s. This Bodhisattva is an image of Avalokiteśvara – the guide to souls with whose aid humans can be helped towards enlightenment. The pose shows the formal gesture of teaching, the right hand raised; the left (now missing) would have lain palm upward on his knee. The headdress, crowning his blue hair, contains the miniature figure of the Amitabha Buddha, the image of the historic Buddha who could be evoked even after his Nirvana. The third, all-seeing, 'eye' is central in his forehead. A major acquisition, achieved in 1982 with help from the National Art-Collections Fund, the Victoria and Albert Museum Purchase Grant Fund and the Friends of the Ashmolean Museum, this serenely dominant colossal presence now presides over the galleries of Eastern Art, and provides a compelling focus for the collections.

▼**32** Chinese: *Horse*, earthenware cast from a mould with traces of slip colour, 35.7 cm high, mid 9th century. A fine example of the many tomb models of horses and other domestic animals that have survived from the T'ang Dynasty. This type of horse, in life larger than the native Chinese pony, and highly valued, was an import from Ferghana. Such figures became much sought after for western collectors in the 20th century, and there were many forgeries. From the Sir Herbert Ingram gift, 1956.

▲ **34** Chinese: *Stemmed bowl*, 16.8 cm high, Ching-techen, mid 14th century. The body is white porcelain, decorated with underglaze blue. The use of a pure cobalt blue perhaps followed the Middle Eastern example, but it was known in Chinese pottery as early as the 8th century. By the time this bowl was made, probably about the time of the foundation (1368) of the Ming dynasty, the technique of its application under glaze on porcelain had reached a very high level of sophistication, which was later especially promoted by a Ming imperial porcelain 'factory' established in 1402 in Ching-techen. This bowl is a charming and brilliant example, of the first quality; it is part of the Sayce bequest.

► **35** Chinese: *Red lacquer dish*, 54.3 cm diameter, 15th century (Ming period). An outstanding example of Chinese lacquer work, spectacular in its unusual size and in the quality of the carving of the floral design. It was acquired in 1980–1 with funds from the bequest of Eric North, complementing very happily the collection of lacquer that he had helped so generously to build up.

◄36 Indian, Gandhāra: *Seated Bodhisattva*, grey schist, polished, 56 cm high, 1st century, from near Hoti Mardan, Gandhāra (part of which is now in Pakistan, and part in Afghanistan). It probably adorned a large *stupa* (the dome-shaped monument characteristic of early Buddhism). The begging-bowl on the base is flanked by two worshippers, perhaps the donors. The dress is such as a prince of the region would have worn. Iconography and pose belong to the Indian tradition, the ritual pose of hands signifying preaching, in this case the Buddhist *dharma* or Law. The style however bears the clear stamp of Graeco-Roman influence. The halo is of Middle Eastern origin, and the two narrow bands that extend out from the turban have been interpreted as derivations from the knotted ends of the Greek diadem. Given by Mrs Gooding, before 1914.

▲ 37 Indian, Mathurā, Uttar Pradesh: *Head of Śiva*, red sandstone, 30.5 cm high, late 4th/early 5th century (Gupta dynasty). This austerely monumental example of Gupta sculpture was probably part of a *linga* (the phallic icon of Śiva); central in the forehead is the 'third eye', symbolically the seat of Śiva's fire of destruction. Acquired in 1939 with the help of Mr and Mrs H.N. Spalding and the National Art-Collections Fund.

◄**38** Indian: *Stater*, gold, 1.9 cm diameter (enlarged almost twice), late 4th/early 5th century. The Gupta kings showed themselves on their gold coins in various roles: here Chandragupta II (reigned 380–414) is dramatically recorded as lion slayer. Given by J.B. Elliott, 1859.

▶**39** Indian: *Muhur*, gold, 2.5 cm diameter (enlarged almost twice), Agra, 1611. A superb example of the exploitation by the Mughal Emperors in India of the decorative possibilities of Persian script. This reverse side records the emperor's name – Jahangir – his lineage and his title. The obverse gives the month (Bahman, the eleventh Persian month), year, and mint.

▶**40** Indian: *Floral carpet*, wool and silk, 210.8 × 147.3 cm. Lahore or Agra, early 18th century. Indian Mughal carpets derived from Persia, although they seem to have some affinities with Turkish carpets. The art of making them was introduced into India probably by the Emperor Akbar (reigned 1556–1605). The finest surviving examples date from the mid 17th century; by the 18th century designs were becoming simpler and more rigid, but the supreme technical quality persisted. The dark wine-red field of this carpet is characteristic, and the green lotus leaf or pod scrolling with dark pink lotuses in the main border stripe proclaims its Indian origin. The warp and weft are of silk; the pile is of goat hair taken from the underside of the throat and neck, which accounts for the particularly fine 'silky' texture. Purchased with the help of the beneficiaries of Sir David Ross, the Victoria and Albert Museum Purchase Grant Fund, and the Friends of the Ashmolean.

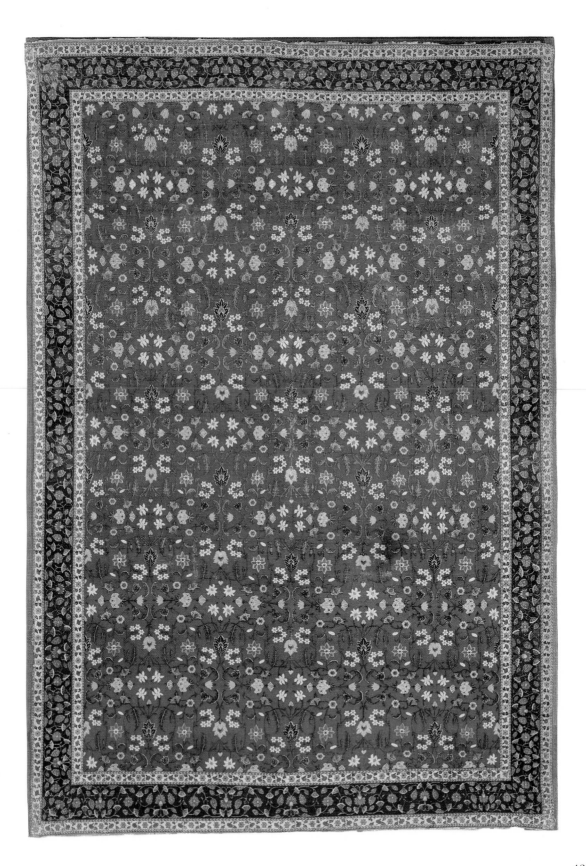

▲ **41** Iranian (Kashan): *Lustre bowl*, artificial paste body, 20 cm diameter. Notable not only because it is dated – 608 M (1211–12) – but as an excellent example of Islamic potters' skill in matching the design, of maidens by a stream, into the shape of the circular, curving bowl. Through Hispano-Moresque ware lustre on tin-glaze was to become the key in the development of Maiolica, Europe's earliest type of decorative glazed ceramics. Given by Sir Alan Barlow, 1956.

▲**42** Islamic (Egypt): *Mosque lamp*, enamelled and gilded glass, 31 cm high, early 14th century. A fine example of the traditional form of the hanging lamps used in mosques. Made for a religious building of Sultan Muhammad ibn Qala'un (1294–1340), and inscribed in his name. Acquired in 1972 with the aid of the Friends of the Ashmolean.

◄**43** Indian (Mughal): *Amīr Hamza overthrows Amīr 'Imad Kāruba*, painting on cloth, 49.95 × 32 cm, *c.*1562. The Amir Hamza, an uncle of the Prophet Muhammad, was a hero of the early battles of Islam. His fantastic adventures were recorded in the narrative cycle of the *Hamza Nāmeh*. The many illustrators of this vast project, which was initiated by Akbar and became one of the most important of all Indian illustrated manuscripts, were directed by two Persian masters. Nonetheless, the vigour and scale of this painting, one of the earliest in this now scattered series in which the basic Mughal style was formed, already show a revolutionary departure from the Persian tradition. From Gerald Reitlinger's gift, 1978.

▼**45** Iranian: *Ewer*, white soft paste porcelain, 21.5 cm high, early 18th century. A wine jug, a most elegant example of the so-called Gombroon ware (from Gombroon, now Bandar Khumeini, on the Persian Gulf, there was brisk export to Europe). The relatively plain style, here with incised designs half-veiled under the glaze, has always coexisted with the richly emphatic and polychrome taste in Islamic culture. Given by Sir Frank Brangwyn.

▼**44** Iranian: *Dinar*, gold, 2.2 cm diameter, early 4th century. A fine portrait of a Sassanian king of Persia, Shapur II (reigned 307–9). The usual Persian monetary standard was silver, and gold coins are rare.

48

◄46 Giotto di Bondone (1267–1337): *Virgin and Child*, panel 28.5 × 19.7 cm. Giotto is traditionally celebrated as the founder of the modern school of painting, and described as of the Florentine School, though he also worked in Padua, Assisi, Rimini and Naples. This painting is universally agreed to be of very high quality, and is ascribed by some to Giotto's own hand; or it may be by one of the collaborators who worked with him in the Lower Church at Assisi in the first decade of the 14th century. Bought by J.R. Anderson (who was much influenced by Ruskin's views on art) in Perugia in 1887, and presented by his widow in 1931.

▲47 Bicci di Lorenzo (1373–1452): *St Nicholas of Bari rebuking the storm*, panel, 29 × 59 cm. Originally part of the predella of an altarpiece painted *c.*1433 for S. Niccolò in Caffagio, Florence; the central panel, of the Virgin and Child, is now at Parma, and others are in the Metropolitan Museum, New York, at Cracow and elsewhere. The style is markedly influenced by the shift from the austerity of Giotto to the more animated, sophisticated manner of the International Gothic. The composition is taken very closely from Gentile da Fabriano's polyptych painted in 1425. The saint (as recorded in the *Golden Legend*) swoops to rescue the imperilled ship, bringing clear weather and a host of stars.

◄48 Domenico Ghirlandaio (1448/9–94): *Portrait of a young man*, panel, 39 × 27.7 cm, probably *c.*1475. For long attributed to Pintoricchio, but current opinion favours Ghirlandaio. This is a variation on a favourite Italian theme of the late 15th century – youth in melancholy; but it is an outstanding, very individual characterisation, elegiac yet entirely lucid. Part of the Fox-Strangways gift, 1850.

▼49 Paolo Uccello (*c.*1396/7–1475): *Hunt in the forest*, panel, complete painting 73.5 × 177 cm, detail shown here approx. 36 × 57 cm, *c.*1465–70. A detail from the most celebrated of the early Italian paintings in the Museum, a masterpiece of Uccello's late style. Huntsmen and hounds in full cry (almost audible) after stags through a darkling wood (trees trimmed to allow mounted hunters free passage), with a crescent moon faint above. Somewhat similar paintings of this date customarily adorned marriage chests (*cassoni*), but this one is too large and its original purpose is unknown, as are the identities of the hunters, but it was probably connected with the circle of Lorenzo de' Medici in Florence. Part of the Fox-Strangways gift, 1850.

◄50 Florentine school: *The Annunciation*, panel, 64.6 × 47.5 cm, perhaps *c*.1430. This magisterially composed and beautifully preserved painting has always been the subject of scholarly argument, attributed variously to Sienese, Florentine, Lombard, and Umbrian origins, and even suspected of Spanish connections. Most recently, a cogent case has been formulated, though not yet generally accepted, for its being a very early work of Uccello (see **49**). The style is very much that of the International Gothic (which Uccello was to modulate markedly in his later manner), but with unusual elements. God the Father despatches the Archangel Gabriel from the top left corner, to materialise life-scale as he kneels before the Virgin, to deliver his fateful message. The despatch is a rare subject, the splendid fanfare on trumpets and other instruments from the serried celestial angels less so. The astonishing unfaded blue of the structure in whose shelter the Virgin sits is perhaps pure ultramarine, most precious of pigments. Acquired by Fox-Strangways before 1850.

►51 Piero di Cosimo (1461/2–1521): *The forest fire*, panel, complete painting 71.2 × 202 cm, details shown here approx. 44 × 33 cm (above), 61 × 75 cm (below). This painting is generally believed to have been part of a series, inspired in part perhaps by an account of man's discovery of fire by the Roman writer Vitruvius, illustrating the history of primordial man. Vasari records the series as decorations by Piero for the house of Francesco del Pugliere, an important Florentine, but already (1568) dispersed. They dated probably from about 1505. Two, *The hunt*, and *The return from the hunt*, are in the Metropolitan Museum, New York, a third, *Hylas and the nymphs*, in the Wadsworth Athenaeum, Hartford, Connecticut, and a fourth, *Vulcan and Aeolus*, at Ottawa. Our painting appears to be the central piece, depicting man somewhat advanced in agriculture, although the central emphasis is on the flight of beasts and birds from the blaze rather than man's taming of fire for his own purposes. The animals comprise a vivid range from the domestic kind to mythological creatures, half-beast, half-man. Presented by the National Art-Collections Fund, 1933.

◀**52** Roger van der Weyden (*c*.1397–1464): *Study of the head of an old man*, silver-point on vellum, 8.4 × 7.6 cm. The authorship of this drawing is much debated, but its fine quality has never been questioned. It appears to relate closely to the head of St Joseph in a Nativity in the altarpieces known as the Granada and Miraflores altars. Acquired in 1935.

▶**53** Hans Holbein the Elder (*c*.1465–1524): *Head of a woman*, silver-point with red chalk and pen on paper, 8.1 × 9 cm. On the other side of the sheet is a study of a man reading, related to the artist's Kaisheim altarpiece at Munich, dated 1502. Drawings by Holbein the Elder are fairly rare, but in quality can be comparable with those of his still more famous son, Hans Holbein the Younger. This beautifully contemplative image was a notable addition to the small but excellent representation of German drawing in the Museum, acquired with the aid of the National Art-Collections Fund and the Victoria and Albert Museum Purchase Grant Fund in 1972.

▶**54** Giovanni Bellini (*c*.1430/1–1516): *St Jerome reading in a landscape*, panel, 27 × 22 cm. A great benefactor of the Ashmolean, C.D.E. Fortnum, bought this picture in Florence in 1864 as being by Basaiti; subsequent scholars have argued copiously over its authorship. At the time of writing, the consensus appears to be for Bellini, but argument should not be allowed to impair anyone's appreciation of the superb quality of this image (labels may change, but the picture remains the same). It was Bellini's example that drew Venetian painters from attachment to belated Gothic into the full stream of Italian Renaissance painting. His many pupils included Giorgione and Titian (see **55–6**). St Jerome and his attendant lion proved an irresistibly attractive subject for many painters of the early Renaissance. Here the lion, certainly tamed, seems to suggest almost shyly to his master, who is absorbed in the good book, that it is dinner time. Beyond, the serene landscape of the Veneto, crystalline in the late light, has a characteristic quality of meditation, both lyrical and elegiac, that heralds the mood of the tragically short-lived Giorgione and the young Titian. The same landscape appears, somewhat prosaically rendered, in a painting (now in Boston) attributed to Jacopo da Valenzia.

◄ 55 Giorgione (Giorgio da Castelfranco, 1478?–1510): *Virgin and Child with a view of Venice beyond*, panel 76.6 × 60.2 cm. Ascribed to Giorgione by the time it reached the collection of the Duc de Tallard early in the 18th century, this is now accepted by many authorities as one of the rare paintings from Giorgione's own hand. The composition derives essentially from treatments of the same theme by his great predecessor and mentor in Venice, Giovanni Bellini, but the topographical background is very unusual. It is a condensed impression of the Molo at Venice and nearby buildings, including the Campanile, the Torre dell' Orlogio, St Mark's and the Doge's Palace. The Campanile, struck by lightning in 1489, is shown with its rebuilding incomplete. Reconstruction was not completed till after Giorgione's death; suggestions for the date of the painting vary between 1500 and 1510. The characterisations of the Virgin and Child, the colour range and the quality in general (though the painting is probably not finished in some areas) seem to agree well with the mere seven paintings virtually universally acknowledged as by Giorgione himself, while the setting is indisputably of Giorgione's home territory.

▲ 56 Titian (Tiziano Uccellio, c.1480/5–1576): *A horse and rider falling*, black chalk on grey paper (squared in red chalk), 27.4 × 26.2 cm. The Venetians of the 16th century, the supreme colourists, did not lay the emphasis on drawing, the linear contour, that other schools did, notably at Florence. Drawings by Titian are fairly rare, and he probably roughed out his compositions straight on to the canvas. At their best however, as in this one, the free, very broad handling of soft chalk can convey a sense of volume, of physical substance and weight that can be positively colouristic. This study almost certainly relates to the lost painting of the Battle of Spoleto executed for the Doge's Palace in Venice in 1537/8 but destroyed in 1577 and known now only by copies. The inscription on it, *Titiano*, is perhaps in the hand of one his greatest admirers, Van Dyck; later owners included Benjamin West and Sir Thomas Lawrence.

58

◄57 Raphael (Raffaello Santi, 1483–1520): *Studies of the heads of two apostles and their hands*, black and white chalk on paper, 49.9 × 36.4 cm. The Ashmolean's collection of drawings by Raphael mostly came to Oxford in 1845/6, when part of Sir Thomas Lawrence's magnificent collection of Old Master drawings was saved by a body of subscribers headed by the 2nd Earl of Eldon, and presented to the University. It is also the largest (over 70) and most representative body of drawings by Raphael in any one institution, and the most spectacular of all is this magisterial cartoon of the two apostles, the young St John the Evangelist and St Peter, for Raphael's last painting before his premature death, *The Transfiguration*, in the Vatican. It relates very closely to the two figures as realised in the painting. Raphael divided his composition into two: the transfigured Christ in the upper region, with the healing of the possessed boy below. The painting was completed after Raphael's death, by his pupils, but the lower half is held to be virtually entirely his. The drawing relates to that part: the two men are mesmerised by loving wonder and compassion at the miracle taking place before their eyes – a union of naturalistic observation and ideal representation almost no less miraculous.

▼58 Michelangelo (Buonarroti, 1475–1564): *Crucifixion*, black chalk on paper, 27.8 × 23.4 cm. The very dark smudges, almost like wounds, were originally the artist's emendations in a white chalk that has now oxidised. Drawn about 1554–7, it is one of an intensely moving series of studies of this subject that obsessed and tormented Michelangelo in the last years of his long life. Compared with his earlier drawings, they seem almost groping in technique, yet they convey an intensity of emotion perhaps rivalled only by Rembrandt. Here Mary (to the right of the cross, not, as is usual, to the left) appears convulsed in her agony. The other figure, St John (so very different from Raphael's image), is shown naked, and has been described as like 'a murderer tormented by his conscience' – and surely Michelangelo, in his overwhelming sense of guilt before God in his last years, identified with him. This, like the Ashmolean's other Michelangelo drawings, came to Oxford from Sir Thomas Lawrence's collection in the same way as the Raphaels, in 1845/6.

◄59 'Matthias Grünewald', *c.*1475–1528: *An elderly woman with clasped hands*, charcoal on black chalk on paper, 37.7 × 23.6 cm, *c.*1520. Very few drawings by Grünewald have survived. This (from the Douce collection) is one of the most striking of them, entirely characteristic of his sinewy style, and of about the same date as his Tauberbischofsheim Crucifixion at Karlsruhe. The ink inscription (early, though not in the artist's hand) identifies the drawing as by 'Mathis von Ossenberg', and is a crucial link in the evidence that established the real name, Mathis Nithart, called Gothart, of one of the greatest geniuses of German art, now universally known as Grünewald. His masterpiece is the famous Isenheimer altarpiece at Colmar. The subject of our drawing is uncertain, perhaps not a study for a Virgin Mary at the cross or a Magdalen, but for a figure attendant in a *Pietà*.

▲60 Albrecht Dürer (1471–1528): *Landscape*, watercolour on paper, 21 × 31.2 cm. This is now generally agreed to be a view of the Val de Cembra, between Cembra and Segonzano, taken on the artist's outward journey from Nüremberg to Venice, his first Italian trip, in 1494. The rare surviving watercolours by Dürer anticipate with startling vividness the achievement of watercolourists working direct from nature three centuries and more later. Though brought to different degrees of finish in various areas of the drawing, this one is amongst his most remarkable masterpieces. From the Chambers Hall gift, 1855.

◄61 Agnolo Bronzino (Agnolo di Cosimo, 1503–72): *Portrait of Giovanni de' Medici* (1543–62), panel, 66.2 × 52.8 cm. Bronzino was the quintessential recorder of the sophisticated persons of the Medici family and their circle in Florence in the mid 16th century, and the supreme Italian master of mannerist court-portraiture: aloof, exquisitely polished surfaces yielding no intimacies but superlative expressions of aristocratic pride and confidence. Our sitter was the second son of Cosimo I de' Medici and Eleanora of Toledo, and destined for the Church perhaps in hope of emulating his Medici forebear, Pope Leo X; though he never took holy orders, he was a Cardinal by 1560, and an Archbishop by 1561 – but died the year after, aged 19. A closely related portrait, in which the sitter has the same dress and pose but a different hairstyle and appears slightly younger, is at Bowood (colln Marquess of Lansdowne); in that version the book has a Greek text from Isocrates, often cited in Renaissance advice to princes. Our portrait shows the boy aged perhaps 8 or 9 (about 1551–2), though few people might be likely to pat his head in anticipation of a gratified response. Acquired by Fox-Strangways before 1850. The frame is contemporary, though married recently to the painting. It is similar to one said to have been designed by Vasari on a painting of the Holy Family, in Florence (colln Sir Harold Acton). The significance of the little allegorical figures painted in monochrome in the medallions is as yet undeciphered.

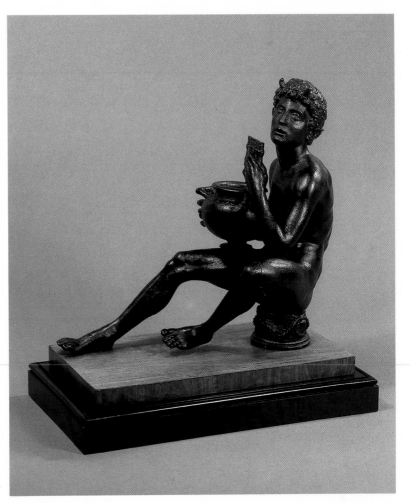

▲62 North Italian school: *Inkstand: Pan listening to an echo*, bronze, 19.7 × 26 cm, first half (?) of the 16th century. This is one of the true masterpieces in bronze of the early 16th century, and for long its sheer quality suggested the name of the great Paduan craftsman, Riccio, as its artist. Present-day intensification and refinement of research into the formidably difficult problem of both attribution and dating of Renaissance bronzes, while revealing ever more definitively the superb quality of the Pan, has yet to agree on its maker. Some of the most beautiful bronzes of the period served humble purposes (knockers, door stops even), as here with Pan, listening, rapt, for the echo over his ink pot. The Museum owes the rich nucleus of what is now one of the finest collections in Europe of such works to the bequest of C.D.E. Fortnum. He bought Pan in Genoa, in 1848, for £10.

►64 Alessandro Allori (1535–1607): *Portrait of a young man*, panel, 133 × 104 cm. From the Rosebery collection at Mentmore, where it was ascribed to Bronzino and the sitter was identified as Benvenuto Cellini. It is signed by Alessandro Allori, and dated 1561 – Allori was Bronzino's foremost pupil in Florence, and developed his master's style in mannerist portraiture in a somewhat less austere mode, though always formal and elegantly aristocratic in expression. Our sitter is still unidentified (possibly connected with the Medici circle), but evidently a collector. Conceivably the medal that he holds and the allegorical emblems, on medallions inset in the edge of the table and on the arm of the chair, may eventually provide clues as to his identity. Further investigation may also decipher what was originally in our picture's background: alterations on the left-hand side are clearly visible to the naked eye. The statuette on the table represents Apollo with his lyre. The mysterious rather Michelangelesque half-naked man seen from behind through the embrasure, looking out over a landscape, occurs again in a very similar portrait of another collector of 1562 (perhaps originally a pair to this one), formerly in the Watney collection. This portrait, bought in 1982 with generous help from the Victoria and Albert Museum Purchase Grant Fund, the National Art-Collections Fund and the Friends of the Ashmolean, has found an ideal setting amongst the Museum's splendid Fortnum collection of Italian bronzes and its later Italian Renaissance paintings.

▲63 Florentine: *Ewer*, white porcelain, Medici ware, decorated in rich blue with sprays of foliage and flowers, 17.8 cm high, *c.*1580. C.D.E. Fortnum, who bequeathed this to the Museum in 1899, had bought it in Naples in 1879 for £60; it came from the Montalto family in Bergo degli Albizzi, who were connections of the Medici. It is one of the most precious of the rare survivals from the Medici establishment, where a variety of soft-paste porcelain was manufactured for the first time in Europe, set up in the late sixteenth century. It bears the factory mark, the letter F (for Firenze) and the outline of the dome of the Cathedral.

65

◀65 Isaac Oliver (*c.*1560/5–1617): *Portrait of an unknown man*, body colours on vellum, 68 × 49 cm, inscribed by the artist in gold *Anno Domini 1588 Ae Suae. 71.* The identity of the old man so brilliantly characterised here is still elusive (an old inscription on the back of the 18th-century(?) frame, 'Lord Bacon', cannot be correct). As a child Oliver came to London from Rouen with his parents, Huguenot refugees: his father was a goldsmith, and at some point Isaac worked with the great English-born miniaturist, Nicholas Hilliard. By the late 1580s Oliver rivalled his master in quality, but was already developing his own style, more down-to-earth, using shadow: here the elegant calligraphy recalls Hilliard's practice, but Oliver was not yet patronised by the court and the sitter could be a member of the foreign community of merchants and craftsmen settled in London, a Dutchman (as in another miniature of Oliver's the same year) or a Frenchman. Purchased with the aid of the Victoria and Albert Museum Purchase Grant Fund, the National Art-Collections Fund, and the Friends of the Ashmolean, 1979.

◀66 English: *Henry VIII*, gold medal, 5.6 cm diameter (here enlarged by about one-third). Known as the 'Supremacy of the Church', this was probably struck by Henry Basse at the London Mint in 1545, ten years after the formal proclamation of Henry VIII as Supreme Head of the Church of England. A vivid and unusual portrait of the King, to compare with the image of him more generally broadcast by copies after Holbein.

▲67 Genoese: *Basin and ewer*, silver, repoussé with some applied castings, the basin 50.5 cm diameter, the ewer 46 cm high. The basin is dated (in a shield held by one of the tritons) 1619; the arms on both places appear to be those of the Lomellini family in Genoa. The cartouches on the rim of the basin feature the loves of Jupiter, Danaë, Olympias, Leda and Semele. In the bowl, a sea battle between nude warriors on sea horses, tritons and nereids, against a background perhaps showing the Ligurian coast, is depicted with great vivacity and subtlety. On the central boss, behind the figure of Victory crowning Neptune, rises the landmark of the Lanterna of Genoa, or Torre di Farro. The ewer has a handle with the young Hercules astride its top, cartouches showing Venus and Cupid, and Mars, on the

shoulder, and on the body, in high relief, the triumph of Neptune and Amphitrite. Both pieces formed part of a set now dispersed between the Ashmolean, Birmingham City Art Gallery, and the Victoria and Albert Museum. Superb examples of the goldsmith's craft in its most exuberant and most sophisticated quality, they may originally have celebrated a marriage, though their early history is unknown till they were bought by the 5th Earl of Shaftesbury in Naples in 1807. They added a spectacular element to the Museum's already rich holding of plate (especially Huguenot silver), when acquired with the aid of the Victoria and Albert Museum Purchase Grant Fund, the National Art-Collections Fund, and the Friends of the Ashmolean in 1974.

◄68 Sir Anthony van Dyck (1599–1641): *The Deposition*, canvas, 207 × 137 cm. Christ has been lowered from the cross, and is supported by Mary and St John, with the Magdalen in prayer behind. It was probably painted during Van Dyck's second Antwerp period, about 1630 – the collapse of Christ's body may owe something to Rubens's great *Descent from the cross* at Antwerp. Van Dyck's unrelentingly intense treatment of the appalling physical destruction inflicted by crucifixion is however essentially his own, though it conveys a starkly tragic feeling that is rare in his work. Given by C.T. Maud, 1869.

▲69 Sir Peter Paul Rubens (1577–1640): *Study of a nude male torso*, charcoal heightened with white, on paper, 31.5 × 36.7 cm. A superb study from the life, and an outstandingly strong and vital example of Rubens's draughtsmanship. It probably relates to the *Raising of the cross*, a subject Rubens treated at least twice; he adapted the pose for several different works, and it may derive from a memory of the antique marble group, *The wrestlers*, found in Rome in 1583 and now in the Uffizi. Chambers Hall gift, 1855.

▼**70** Rembrandt van Rijn (1606–69): *Saskia asleep in bed*, pen and brush in bistre on paper, 13.7 × 20.3 cm. Probably *c*.1635; the inscription *Renbrant* is later, but this is undoubtedly one of the masterpieces of Rembrandt's own hand. It was drawn in perhaps a few minutes, with breathtaking speed and virtuosity in control of contrast of different tones of the bistre wash, of the broad brush and the sharp quill-pen, and of light and shade. It records his young wife Saskia, asleep – perhaps suffering from one of her frequent ailments, but here evoked deathless by her husband's genius. Acquired 1954.

►**71** David de Heem (*c*.1570–1632): *Still-life of fruit*, canvas, 28 × 23 cm, signed, *c*.1630. Grapes, a peach, nectarines, cherries, blackberries, a white butterfly and a bee make up this fine example from the great collection of Dutch and Flemish still-life pictures in the Daisy Linda Ward Bequest, 1940. This is one of the most comprehensive collections of the genre ever brought together, with examples of many of the major and minor painters of the time, many signed and dated. In this one, David de Heem (one of the dynasty of painters of that surname) seems to have abandoned any overt allegorical references, such as were often popular in still-life and flower paintings, and to be simply luxuriating in the sensual delight of high summer's abundance – a theme with special appeal for Dutch burghers in the long, cold and dark winters of the Netherlands.

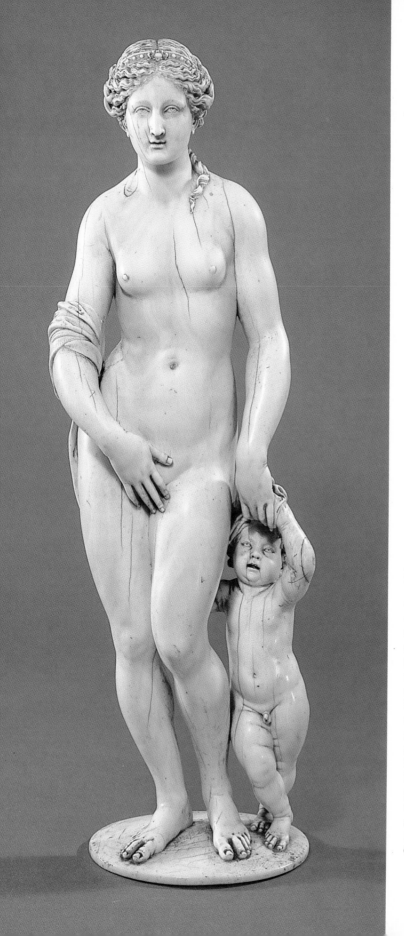

◀72 Georg Petel (1590/1–1633/4): *Venus and Cupid*, statuette, ivory, 40.5 cm high, signed on the base *Jorg Petl. f.* A superlative example of German small-scale sculpture of the early 17th century, once in the collection of Rubens, who may have acquired it from the sculptor. Petel worked in Rome and Flanders as well as his home town of Augsburg, and this statuette can perhaps be dated *c.*1624, when he and Rubens were both in Antwerp. It was bought by George Villiers, 1st Duke of Buckingham, from Rubens's collection, and ultimately was one of the most prized acquisitions (1932) made for the Museum by Sir Kenneth (Lord) Clark when he was a Keeper in the Ashmolean.

▶73 English: *Adam and Eve goblet*, baluster glass with diamond engraving, 27 cm high, late 17th century. The very rich decoration shows Adam and Eve with the tree of knowledge and the serpent, amongst the beasts of the field and the birds of the air. The two figures derive from an engraving by P. Stent. Other glasses engraved with the same subject are known, but none of this quality. Given by Mr and Mrs H.R. Marshall, who are best known for the superb Marshall collection of Worcester porcelain, but who also endowed the Museum with some fine specimens of English glass (through the National Art-Collections Fund, 1956).

74 Nicolas Poussin (1594–1665): *The exposition of Moses*, canvas, 150 × 204 cm, 1654. When the Israelites were in exile in Egypt, the Pharaoh ordered that any male child born to a Hebrew woman be put to death (Exodus 1). The mother of the infant Moses preferred secretly to entrust her child in a basket of bullrushes to whatever mercy the river Nile might bring. When the daughter of Pharaoh came down to wash herself in the river, she found the basket, 'And when she had opened it, she saw the child: and behold, the babe wept. And she had compassion on him . . .'. Poussin painted the happy outcome several times, but the tragic moment of abandonment only twice, the second time in this sombre masterpiece. In his later years Poussin's paintings tend to darken in mood. Here the austere restraint of gesture of the despairing parents as they leave the baby is typical, and the setting is composed as a generalised expression of antique dignity, an ideal city of the Pharaohs. It brings together great monuments redolent of classical antiquity – the Castel S. Angelo at Rome, the pyramid of Cestius, and the temple of the Vestals at Tivoli, following Piranesi's reconstruction; a specific Egyptian location is indicated by the Sphinx near the water's edge. Poussin painted this for the painter Jacques Stella. It served as design for a Gobelins tapestry. Later it was in the great collection of the Duc d'Orléans. It came to England following the dispersal of that collection after the French Revolution, and was finally acquired by the Museum, aided by the generosity of members of the Fry family, in 1950.

▲ **75** Claude Lorrain (Gellée) (1602–82): *Landscape, with Ascanius shooting the stag of Sylvia*, canvas, 120 × 150 cm, signed below in the centre and dated *A ROMAE 1682*. The incident was taken from Virgil, *Aeneid* Book 7: after the landing of the Trojans in Latium, Ascanius, son of Aeneas, sighted a splendid stag ('his antlers entwined with delicate garlands'), stretched his bow and shot it. The stag belonged to Sylvia, daughter of the master of the herds of King Latinus, and the incident sparked off the war between the Trojans and the Latins. The painting was commissioned by Prince Onofrio Lorenzo Colonna, Grand Constable of the Kingdom of Naples but living in Rome, and came to England from the Palazzo Colonna in 1798/9. It was Claude's last painting; he died in Rome in November 1682. Subject and setting – classical mythology in an ideal classical landscape with its temple, obviously reflecting the artist's almost life-long love affair with the Roman countryside – are typical, as are the exaggeratedly elongated human figures. The markedly blue tonality, however, is most unusual: it seems – appositely and movingly – almost crepuscular. The painting may be unfinished, and Claude may have intended to modify this tonality in the final revision more towards the serenely sun-infused atmosphere with which his work is always associated. It remains a convincing and hauntingly beautiful climax to his life's achievement. Given by Mrs W.F.R. Weldon in 1926; the Museum also possesses one of Claude's drawings for the picture.

76 Japanese: *Powder flask*, lacquer on wood, 15.7 cm high, *c.*1600 (Momoyama). When the Portuguese arrived in Japan in 1542, the first Westerners, their personal habits, extraordinary European clothes, stature, and colouring, together with two most important imports previously unknown, Christianity and guns, caused great astonishment. This attractive little object is a flask to hold the black gunpowder for muskets. The rich brown lacquer is decorated with a Japanese view of the absurd exotic foreigners to whom Japan owed the introduction of fire-power. On one side a man stoops to admire some flowers, accompanied by an immensely tall figure draped in an ankle-length cloak. The man on the side shown here wears a tall red hat and an exaggerated version of the enormously baggy trousers in fashion in Europe at the time. The images suggest that the Japanese, always delighting in caricature, saw their visitors as such; present-day Europeans may be reminded of the style of Aubrey Beardsley. Examples of this type of lacquer are extremely rare, and acquisition of the flask was aided by the generosity of the Friends of the Ashmolean.

77 Korean: *Large storage jar*, porcelain with underglaze decoration in iron and cobalt blue, 39.7 cm high, late 17th century (Choson dynasty). A clear Korean departure from the Chinese porcelain tradition, in its globular shape and superb brushwork in the grape-vine motif that encompasses the whole diameter. Given by Mr and Mrs K.R. Malcolm in memory of their son John Malcolm, Scholar of Worcester College (died 1974).

▼ **78** Iranian: *Dish, with quails*, soft-paste porcelain, decorated in blue under a colourless glaze, 44.5 cm high. A charming example of Safavid blue and white ware of about 1700–25, its seven quails decoratively dispersed within a meander border. It came with Gerald Reitlinger's gift to the Museum (1978): the Islamic section of his great collection was as important as the Chinese and Japanese ones, and, typically, he was especially interested in the inter-relationship of Chinese and Near Eastern ceramics.

◄79 Edward Pierce (*c*.1635–95): *Sir Christopher Wren* (1632–1723), marble bust, 66 cm high, 1673. Given to the University of Oxford by Christopher, the son of the sitter, in 1737. Portrait busts, other than for funerary monuments, were still extremely rare in this period, and this is probably the finest baroque bust ever carved in England. No other portrait of Wren catches him in anything but the settled dignity of the establishment; this one, in its quick and eager vitality, answers the versatile genius of the young sitter, brilliant mathematician and great architect. Pierce worked for Wren as a sculptor, notably in St Paul's and the exuberance of this bust and the sophistication of the treatment, especially in the hair, suggest that Wren himself, who had seen Bernini's work when he visited Paris in 1665, may have had some influence on the sculptor's conception and approach. Pierce's bust of Oliver Cromwell, also in the Museum, is by comparison a very dour and staid affair. Plaster casts derived from the Wren bust are to be found elsewhere, for example at All Souls College, and at the Royal Academy, London.

►80 Antonio Stradivari (1644?–1737): *Violin*, 59.3 cm long, Cremona, with the original label: *Antonius Stradivarius Cremoensis/Faciebat Anno 1716*. This is one of the most famous violins in the world, known as the 'Messiah'. One of its owners in the 19th century, Tarisio, boasted about it much but hardly ever produced it, until someone said: 'It's like the Messiah, always promised and never appearing.' The body is believed to be uniquely almost in mint condition, though the neck has been lengthened and the fingerboard is modern. The varnish, thought by some to be crucially important to the tone, has been claimed as the only original varnish to have survived on a Strad. Though Joachim praised the tone, the instrument has been played hardly at all in recent years owing to the demands of conservation. It came to the Museum with the remarkable gift of the Arthur and Alfred Hill collection of musical instruments, 1939.

▲**81** Jean Siméon Chardin (1699–1779): *Still-life*, canvas, 32 × 39 cm. More exactly, 'A Pitcher with Cover, Two Eggs, a Casserole, Three Herrings hanging on a Wall, a Copper Pot, a Slice of Fish on a Pot Cover, and a Jug on a Stone Ledge'. That reads like an assemblage of the basics for a cookery recipe, and so in a sense it is; but the painting, the final result, 'la matière', is indeed perfection for the visual appetite. At the same time the sensual element, the succulence, is underlaid by a most rigorously exact structure, perfectly balanced, curve answering curve, shadow counterpoised against light, the higher tones of the herrings, the salmon slice, and the eggs accentuating the basic browns and greens of the kitchenware. The Frenchman Chardin was very much aware of his great predecessors of the century before in Holland and Flanders, and his earliest still-lifes tend to be more reminiscent of them than is this one, which belongs to a group of the early 1730s – magisterial close-ups, broadly handled. His genius lifted the art of still-life, still in his time considered by critics to be the least important branch of painting, to a level in which its masterpieces are proved equal to those of any other branch. In the 20th century, his heirs are painters like Cézanne or Morandi. Given by Mrs W.F.R. Weldon, 1927.

►**82** Antoine Watteau (1684–1721): *Le repos gracieux*, panel, 19.5 × 11.3 cm. For many people, Watteau's paintings are the quintessence of French rococo painting. He was the creator of a bewitchingly elegant never-never land, but it is a world whose artificiality is belied by intimations of melancholy and transience, and sustained by swift, strong draughtsmanship. This little painting comes probably from relatively early in his career, about 1712, but is infused with the mysterious ambiguity that haunts so much of his work. It could be an incident isolated from a *fête galante*, that convention popular since the 16th century, featuring lovers in an idyllic landscape, sometimes banqueting, sometimes with music. Rubens's *Garden of love* is one of the masterpieces of the genre, and Watteau, himself of Flemish stock (Valenciennes, his birthplace, was only incorporated within France shortly before he was born), was a passionate admirer of Rubens. Our painting seems to represent two actors in costume, the man imploring, the woman still turned slightly away – yet the enchanting garden setting, complete with fountain, seems real rather than a stage-set. Is an erotic scene from a play being pursued by the actors in real life, off-stage? The 'meaning' of Watteau's pictures is so often enigmatic. He drew compulsively, and would often put together in a painting figures based on drawings made perhaps years earlier, composing them like motifs – musical analogies always come to mind. There are related drawings of the King Charles spaniel and the man in this picture at Fontainebleau and Moscow respectively. The mood here is muted, a harmony of soft blacks, grays, whites, a glint of yellow and glow of the pink sash, olive-greens. Given by Mrs W.F.R. Weldon, 1927.

83 Giovanni Battista Piazzetta (1682–1754): *Head of a youth*, black and white chalks on brownish paper, 31.5 × 29.9 cm. A very vigorous example, entirely characteristic, of this Venetian painter's style. Acquired in 1934.

▶**84** Italian: *Scudo*, silver, 4.5 cm diameter (here enlarged almost twice), 1713. Minted for Pope Clement XI, who appears on the obverse. The reverse, shown here, is an admirable example of the Italian delight in encompassing architectural vistas within the miniature confines of a coin or medal. The Piazza del Pantheon in Rome, with obelisk, fountain, and surrounding houses, shops and streets, is depicted as it can be seen today, little changed.

▶**85** Thomas Gainsborough (1727–88): *Miss Gainsborough gleaning*, canvas, 73 × 63 cm. As far as is known, this is the only surviving half of a double portrait that was recorded in the *Somerset House Gazette*, 1824, before the painting was divided: 'his two daughters in the garb of peasant girls on the confines of a cornfield, dividing their gleanings . . . of the ages about eight or nine . . . The painting is pure and the characters are nature, clothed with the utmost simplicity of art. Unfortunately both the pictures [i.e. portraits] are left in part unfinished.' Gainsborough's daughters appear in several of the most enchanting paintings of his early maturity, in the late 1750s. The girl portrayed here is probably the younger, Margaret. The unfinished state of the painting serves to intensify the wistful lyric charm of the child's face. Acquired in 1975, thanks to an anonymous donation in memory of Helen, Henry and Marius Winslow, topped up by a grant from the Victoria and Albert Museum Purchase Grant Fund.

86 James Cox (active from 1749: d.1791/2): *Striking Clock*, 65 cm high. The movement was made in London about 1780 by Cox, and is set in a case of English ormolu, topped by a lion supporting the Stuart arms of England, and decorated below the dial with a miniature painting by J-J. De Gault (*c*.1738–1812). The clock is believed to have been made for Henry Benedict, Cardinal York (1725–1807), self-styled 'Henry IX, King of England', and the last of the Stuarts. The clock came with the bequest of J.F. Mallett in 1947, and still marks passing time in the galleries, and enlivens with its chime. Mallett's bequest created the rich nucleus of the Museum's very important collection of watch cases.

87 Giovanni Battista Tiepolo (1696–1770): *Young woman with a macaw*, canvas, 70 × 52 cm. Tiepolo is famous as the spectacular decorator of palaces in the Veneto, Würzburg, Verona and elsewhere, in which the exhilarating aerial style of the rococo reached a climax; he is less well known for his few small cabinet paintings (other than oil-studies for larger works). This brilliantly and exotically seductive painting is probably of about 1750–60, and, following its acquisition in 1955 (gift of the National Art-Collections Fund from the E.E. Cook collection), rapidly became a prime favourite with visitors to the Museum. A pastel copy of it is at Washington, and the Ashmolean also owns a drawing by Tiepolo of the same subject in a very similar pose, but reversed (engraved, again reversed, by D. Tessari).

David Garrick Esq.
given at Rome
1764.

◄**88** Pompeo Batoni (1708–87): *David Garrick*, canvas, 76 × 63 cm. David Garrick (1717–79), the great actor and impresario whose name is almost synonymous with the English drama of the second half of the 18th century, was in Rome in late 1764 and early spring 1765. He sat to Batoni, the favoured portraitist in Rome of so many British 'grand tourists', during that time, and is shown (no doubt at his own behest) with an illustrated volume of Terence. That very splendid edition was first published in Urbino in 1736; it is open at the engraved page showing the masks from the *Andria*. Garrick's close friend, George Colman, was at the time engaged on a translation of Terence. Later, Garrick gave this portrait to the Rev. Richard Kaye, and it had come to Oxford (to the Bodleian) by 1827. A curious associated item survives in the Museum of London, the velvet coat, deep purplish brown, worn by Garrick for the sittings; a former curator of that Museum claimed that 'when left to itself' it goes into two folds on the left breast, as in the painting.

▲**89** English: *Worcester porcelain*, circular dish, 29.1 cm diameter, square mark, third quarter of the 18th century. The decoration, by J.H. O'Neale, of a mule attacking a seated cavalier and his small dog, is based on an engraving for Fable LXXXI, 'The ass and the little dog', in Barlow's *Aesop* (1687). The dish is one item in the magnificent collection of Worcester porcelain given by Mr and Mrs H.R. Marshall in memory of their only son William Somerville Marshall, of Trinity College, Oxford, killed in action in Holland 26 November 1944.

◄**90** Japanese: *Large jar*, porcelain, decorated in overglaze blue, red, green, yellow, aubergine and black enamels, 35.2 cm high, late 17th century. The design, which is continuous round the jar, shows pavilions and temples set amongst trees and rocky hills. A spectacular specimen of early enamelled ware from the very rich additions by Gerald Reitlinger's gift of 1978 to the Museum's holdings of Japanese porcelain.

▲**91** Watanabe Shiko (1683–1755): *Autumn and winter*, mixed watercolour technique on gold leaf on paper, sixfold screen, each panel 154 × 52 cm. One of a pair of screens, *Flowers of the four seasons*; its companion, *Spring and summer*, is also in the Ashmolean. Work by Watanabe Shiko, to whom these screens are confidently attributed, is fairly rare: though he had great talent and skill, he was never a professional painter but an official of high social status in the service of Lord Konoe Ichiro, attached to the court of the Emperor in Kyoto. His style here shows an eclectic yet individual blending of elements of the preceding Kano style with others that anticipate the Maruyama and Shijo styles, a move from the very formalised towards a greater realism and lighter elegance. Acquired in 1970 with the aid of the Victoria and Albert Museum Purchase Grant Fund and the National Art-Collections Fund.

◄**92** Louis François Roubiliac (1702/5–62): *George Frideric Handel (1685–1759)*, terracotta, 98 cm. This is probably Roubiliac's final model for the full-scale marble monument set up opposite Poets' Corner in Westminster Abbey in 1762. Roubiliac, a Huguenot native of France, brought to England the virtuosity and movement, and also, in portrait characterisation, the naturalism of the finest European rococo sculpture. This monument is far distant from the traditionally pompous mode of funerary sculpture and shows the great composer in everyday dress involved with the composition of his score, humanly credible in posture yet also nobly elegant. Handel points to a figure above with a harp, perhaps the psalmist David, as if claiming inspiration. Given to the University by James Wyatt in 1848.

▼**93** Thomas Rowlandson (?1756–1827): *Radcliffe Square, Oxford*, pen and ink and watercolour on paper, 22 × 31.1 cm. The view (wrongly inscribed as 'Magdalen College') is of All Souls, with the Radcliffe Camera to the left, and is Rowlandson's spirited variation on an engraving by Isaac Taylor after D. Harris published on the *Oxford Almanack* for 1790. The figures, including the stout aged don in the bathchair harassed by the dog, are characteristically and essentially Rowlandson's own. The Museum owns some seventy drawings by Rowlandson, some of them bought direct from the artist by Francis Douce, though this one was given by A.E. Anderson in 1910.

▶**94** Francis Perigal I (active 1741–56): *Watch*, London, *c.*1745. The outer case, shown here is carved from a single piece of reddish, brownish veined agate, mounted in gold cagework (mark of Stephen Goujon). Part of Eric Bullivant's bequest (1974), which strengthened still further the enormously rich collection of watch cases bequeathed by J.F. Mallett (1947).

◄ **95** William Blake (1757–1827): *Dante and Statius sleeping, Virgil watching*, watercolour with pen and ink on paper, 52 × 36.8 cm. The painter John Linnell, friend and patron of Blake, from whose collection this came, commissioned a complete set of illustrations for the *Divine Comedy* from Blake in 1824. Blake died before completing the series. This one illustrates Canto 27, ll. 70–108, of *Purgatory*; the poets rest after passing through the flames guarding the Seventh Circle, Statius below, Dante in the middle, and Virgil leaning on his elbow above. Within the enormous moon appears Dante's vision of Rachel and Leah, the Old Testament types of the active and the contemplative life. A characteristic and beautiful example of Blake's visionary style, it reports what his 'inner eye' saw, but also depends on what his more orthodox eyes had registered – in Michelangelo, in Gothic ogee curves. Given through the National Art-Collections Fund, 1918.

▲ **96** Samuel Palmer (1805–81): *The valley thick with corn*, pen and dark brown ink, brush with sepia mixed with gum on paper, 18.2 × 27.5 cm. Signed and dated 1825, from early in the young artist's 'visionary Shoreham period'. From the mid 1820s to the mid 1830s, Samuel Palmer produced a range of landscapes in a technique peculiar to him, creating from the Kentish countryside round the little village of Shoreham a vision of pastoral luxuriance and abundance. It is far from a literal description, but transposed into what Palmer called 'the ponderous globosity of art'; in mood it is reminiscent of Blake's little woodcut illustrations for Thornton's *Virgil*, conveying an intense mystical apprehension of divinity informing nature. The title comes from Psalm 65; the reclining figure has been connected with Bunyan's Christian, resting half-way up the Hill Difficulty, in *The Pilgrim's Progress*. Acquired in 1941.

▼ **97** John Constable (1776–1837): *Watermeadows near Salisbury*, canvas, 32 × 38 cm. A late study, swift and broad and brilliant in execution, probably of a view from the library windows in the home of Constable's great friend and supporter, Archdeacon Fisher, in the Close of Salisbury Cathedral. It relates closely to two oil sketches in the Victoria and Albert Museum, both painted in July 1829, which is presumably also the date of this more ambitious work. It is a wonderfully fresh example of Constable's power, unknown before him, to snatch down on to canvas an equivalent of English weather that one can almost smell and feel. As 'A valley in the Downs' it came to the Museum as part of Chambers Hall's gift in 1855. Chambers Hall may have bought this scintillating study direct from the artist.

► **98** John Sell Cotman (1782–1842): *Near Brandsby, Yorkshire*, watercolours over pencil on greyish paper, 33 × 22.8 cm, dated 16 July 1805. Cotman's biographer, Sydney Kitson, who bequeathed this drawing in 1938, reproduced it as frontispiece to his biography (1937) of the artist. Kitson suggested that it was unfinished, perhaps 'simply a demonstration to his hostess and her daughters [it was his third, and last, visit to Brandsby] of rapid out of door painting . . . a fascinating example of the translation of an ordinary scene into a patterned harmony at the hands of an inspired artist'. It is a brilliant, unfaded representation of the powers of the great Norfolk watercolourist, in the freshness of his youth.

▲**99** John Robert Cozens (1752–97): *Sepulchral remains in the Campagna*, watercolour on paper, 26 × 37.4 cm. Drawn probably in 1783, looking towards Rome – the ruins in the foreground may be of the Villa of the Quintilii, with the Aqua Claudi on the skyline in the background. The moody weather and the melancholy of classical ruins combine to help create one of the most lyrically atmospheric of all Cozens's masterpieces; it belonged originally to William Beckford, and was bequeathed to the Museum by F.P. Barnard in 1934.

▲ 100 Joseph Mallord William Turner (1775–1851):
Venice, the Grand Canal, watercolour on paper, 21.5 ×
31.5 cm. Drawn in 1840, during Turner's last visit to
Venice. S. Maria della Salute is seen on the right.
This is amongst the finest of his later watercolours,
realised in swiftly fluid, delicate wash of diaphanous
yet brilliant colour, stabilised by very economic pen-
work and anchored in the dark accent of the gondola.
John Ruskin, patron and passionate apologist of
Turner's work, gave this drawing to the University in
1863; he endowed both Oxford and Cambridge (the
Fitzwilliam Museum) with a rich representation of
Turner's watercolours and drawings of all periods.

► 101 John Ruskin (1819–1903): *St Mark's, Venice*,
watercolour on paper, 43 × 29.2 cm, dated 27 May
1846. Sketched after rain. Ruskin's talent as
draughtsman tends to be overshadowed by his
greater fame as writer on a huge variety of subjects.
This drawing was included in the extensive collection
of specimen drawings and other material organised
by him to help students learning to draw, and now
deposited in the Museum.

▲ **102** Jean-Baptiste-Camille Corot (1796–1875):
Landscape: le Petit Chaville, near Ville d'Avray, paper laid
on canvas, 24 × 35 cm. Painted about 1823–5. A
larger version is recorded, painted in 1855 and now
untraced. Ville d'Avray is near Paris, where Corot's
father owned a property. Even in his earliest
paintings he worked out of doors in oils, on small
relatively informal landscapes, as here, developing
his remarkable power of direct but selective
observation. His grasp of the unity of light that he was
to sharpen to such acuity in the simplification of form
and command of space in the crystalline light of Italy,
whither he departed in late 1825, is already
impressive. Some have suggested that a tradition of
classic French landscape, starting with Poussin,
closes in Corot, but also that another, starting with
Corot, takes one through to Cézanne. This picture is
said to have been bought back from its owner by the
artist in 1874; it was in the Corot studio sale after his
death (it bears the studio stamp), and was
bequeathed by F. Hindley-Smith in 1939.

►**103** Sir Francis Chantrey (1781–1841): *William
Wordsworth (1770–1850)*, plaster, 58.4 cm. The model
for a marble bust (now at Indiana University) of the
poet commissioned in 1820 by Sir George Beaumont,
leading patron and arbiter of taste in Regency times,
and a generous benefactor of Wordsworth.
Somewhat idealised ('the soul of the poetry, but not
the countenance of the man', said Coleridge), this is
nevertheless in many ways the most satisfactory,
adequate, portrait of the great romantic poet.
Chantrey, the most successful British sculptor of his
time, kept the models for most of his commissions
(rather as a photographer may keep negatives for
repeat orders); these were all given to the University
by his widow in 1842. This bust is formally conceived
within a plain neo-classic convention, yet succeeds in
conveying very subtly an essentially romantic
quality.

◄**104** Sir John Everett Millais (1829–96): *The return of the dove to the Ark*, canvas, 85 × 55 cm, signed and dated 1851. Wives of the sons of Noah hold the dove that returned to the Ark bearing a sprig of olive, indicating that the waters were subsiding, and dry land near. The painting was exhibited at the Royal Academy in 1851. Gautier, though querying the ages of the wives (surely still in their early teens) was – unexpectedly for a French critic – entranced by it; Ruskin, while characteristically and correctly noting that the olive twig was not olive (presumably not available), was one of several who bid for it at the Royal Academy. However, it had already been bought by a staunch patron of the Pre-Raphaelite painters in their youthful beginnings. Thomas Combe was the University printer at Oxford, and this is one of the important works by members of the Brotherhood that came from his widow to the Museum in 1894. It was the first Pre-Raphaelite painting that William Morris and Burne-Jones were to see, in a window in the High Street, Oxford. It remains one of the most brilliant masterpieces of the original Pre-Raphaelites' ideal. Their style may not (as Gautier observed) remind anyone of that of the early Italian painters who preceded Raphael, but their high moral purpose (Millais' picture can also be read as an allegory of hope), their unpretentious sincerity, and their dedication in the minutest attention (despite the olive) to the detail, colour and structure of nature, could rout stale academicism with the brilliance of their attack.

▲**105** Dante Gabriele Rossetti (1828–82): *Elizabeth Siddal*, pen and black ink on paper, 12.2 × 10.7 cm, with the artist's monogram, and dated 6 February 1855. One of many drawings Rossetti made of Elizabeth during their protracted engagement, and perhaps his most beautiful, conveying with entranced simplicity that melancholy, dreamy, feminine beauty that was the Pre-Raphaelite ideal. She is as if shadowed by premonition of her early death from consumption. The drawing belonged to the artist's brother, W.M. Rossetti, and came to the Museum with F.F. Madan's Bequest, 1961.

▼**106** Arthur Hughes (1832–1915): *Home from the sea*, panel, 50.8 × 65.1 cm. Hughes was one of the earliest followers of the seven Pre-Raphaelite brethren. The picture is signed and dated 1862, but Hughes painted it first in 1856 (the setting being taken from Chingford Church in Essex), adding the figure of the boy's sister (painted from Hughes's young wife) only in 1862. The sailor boy, in his shore-going 'whites', is portrayed on the newly turfed grave of his mother, who has died while he was at sea: one of the most poignant of all Pre-Raphaelite images, in its vivid contrast of youth and the spring foliage with death and grief. Presented by Vernon Watney, 1907.

►**107** Philip Webb (1831–1915) and Sir Edward Burne-Jones (1833–98): *The Prioress's Tale cabinet*, wood, 222 cm high. Designed by Webb in 1857, and decorated by Burne-Jones with scenes from the tale told by the Prioress in *The Canterbury Tales*. Chaucer's portrait (following that in Occleve's manuscript) is shown at the bottom on the right. This was Burne-Jones's first major foray into oil-painting, and formed his wedding present to William Morris at Morris's marriage to Jane Burden in 1858. Morris's daughter May bequeathed it to the Museum in 1939.

▲ **108** Edouard Manet (1833–83): *Le déjeuner sur l'herbe*, pen and ink and watercolour on paper, 37 × 46.8 cm. Very closely related to the once notorious and now world-famous painting (in the Louvre), rejected by the Paris Salon in 1863 but shown amid noisy controversy at the Salon des Refusés; another version of that is in the Courtauld Institute, London. The exact role of our drawing in the evolution of the composition is not yet clear. Manet possibly intended the oil painting as a modern equivalent of the young Titian's *Fête champêtre* in the Louvre, the most famous example of the classic pastoral idyll. French society of the 1860s, however, found the association of the nude female with the two decorously fully clad gentlemen

bizarre and scandalous (the models were Manet's brother, Eugène, and his future brother-in-law Ferdinand Leenhoff; the woman in the final painting was a professional model, Victorine Meurent). But the composition depends primarily and very closely on part of a Renaissance engraving very respectably established in art history, Marcantonio Raimondi's print after Raphael of a *Judgement of Paris*. Our drawing comes from the Cassirer collection, and was one of the distinguished items accepted by the Government from the estate of Dr and Mrs R. Walzer of North Oxford in lieu of tax and allocated, at their request, to the Ashmolean, in 1980.

▼**109** Camille Pissarro (1830–1903): *Le Jardin des Tuileries, temps de pluie*, canvas, 65 × 92 cm, signed and dated 1899. This exquisite and subtly atmospheric impression of the Tuileries garden in Paris, on a grey, wet day, was painted from a window in an upper level of the Rue de Rivoli. Pissarro painted this view more than once, from various angles and in different weathers, towards the end of his life, when he found such urban vistas, seen from above, particularly congenial. He was by now fragile in health, and suffering from trouble with his eyes; but here the vision and the technique of this great founder-member of the Impressionist School show no signs of decay. The Museum has a formidable holding of paintings, drawings, prints and documents by Pissarro that came to it by the generosity of his family, though this one (which had belonged to Camille's son, the painter Lucien, who settled in England) is yet another magnificent witness to Mrs Florence Weldon's acumen and generosity in her bequest in 1937.

▲**110** Edgar Degas (1834–1917): *Three studies of a ballet dancer*, charcoal and pastel on yellowish paper, 39 × 63.8 cm, stamped *Degas*, from the studio sale in 1919. A characteristic attempt by the draughtsman to catch the fleeting poses of the dancers in movement, whom he drew endlessly. Bequeathed by Mrs F.R. Weldon, 1937.

◄**111** Edgar Degas (1834–1917): *Study of a jockey*, black chalk on buff paper, 49.9 × 32.5 cm, stamped *Degas*. This bold, incisive study may relate to Degas' painting *The race course* (Louvre) of about 1876, or may possibly be connected to the well-known *Start of the race* (Dauforth Collection, Providence) of about 1886–90. Bequeathed by John Bryson, 1977.

▼**112** Vincent van Gogh (1853–90): *Restaurant de la Sirène, Asnières*, canvas, 52.5 × 64.5 cm. After groping his tormented way from abortive careers as art-dealer, schoolmaster and lay missionary, Van Gogh started between 1880 and 1885 to find himself in his native Holland as a painter, largely self-taught, of hard-wrought dark landscapes and records of peasant life. Late in 1885, he moved to Antwerp, his palette already beginning to lighten, and then, in two years in Paris from February 1886, he discovered the revolutionary theories and high-keyed colour of the Impressionists, several of whom, notably Toulouse-Lautrec and Gauguin, he came to know well. Like them, he found congenial subject matter in the streets of Paris and in the adjacent countryside. The Restaurant at Asnières, shown in this painting, was a popular resort just out of town on the river, and Van Gogh's treatment of it (probably in early summer 1887) illustrates his new-found command of the

exhilaration of colour, the dazzle of colour in sunlight evoked with a staccato technique of hatch or stipple brush strokes. His style was moving from dark into an exaltation of light, but his life, his mental equilibrium, were not responding so happily. In February 1888 he moved south, to the extraordinary revelation of the Provençal landscape, of Arles, St Rémy, the Saintes-Maries and the Alpilles under the blazing Midi sun, which he was to paint insatiably but which failed to cure the enveloping mental darkness. Barely two years later, he took his own life. A preparatory drawing for this painting is in the Rijksmuseum van Gogh, Amsterdam, and a different view of the Restaurant is in the Louvre. An engaging little drawing of Van Gogh about this time, drawn in Paris by Camille Pissarro's son Lucien in amiable converse with the critic Féneon, also belongs to the Museum. Bequest of Dr Erich Alport, 1982.

▲113 Pablo Picasso (1881–1974): *Blue roofs*, millboard, 40 × 60 cm, signed, painted in 1901. Picasso first left Spain for Paris in October 1900, though he was not to settle there finally till 1904. In May 1901, after winter in Spain, he returned to Paris and to a studio high up at 130ter, Boulevard de Clichy. He was already experimenting with divisionist technique, juxtaposing pure primary colours and complementaries. The *Blue roofs* was painted at this time and exhibited at the Galeries Vollard in the Rue Laffitte. It is the view from his studio window. It can be thought of as recording the excitement of the young desperately poor 19-year-old artist from abroad, a stereotypical view, from a traditionally romantic eyrie, but handled far from traditionally, by an aspiring newcomer to the great city; or as the prelude to the 'Blue Period' of 1902–4, the first of those dizzying, dazzling phases with which the great polymath and innovator in western art was to astonish the world for the next seventy years. Bequeathed by F. Hindley Smith, 1939.

▼**114** Aleksandr Nikolaevich Benois (1870–1960): *Design for the Emperor's bedroom, in 'Le Rossignol'*, body colours on paper, 63 × 97 cm, signed, inscribed and with dates *1914–1917 ... Moscou – St Petersbourg – Paris*. One of eight designs in the Museum by Benois for the Diaghilev production of Stravinsky's opera *Le Rossignol* at the Paris Opera in 1914. Benois considered his *Rossignol* designs to be amongst his masterpieces, and never forgave Diaghilev when he replaced them with new ones by Matisse for a ballet production of Stravinsky's music, in 1920. The donor to the Museum, Mikhail Vasil'evich Braikevitch was a dedicated patron of the ballet and a collector, but he left his first collection in Russia (now in the Museum of Russian Art, Odessa) when he emigrated after the Revolution. His second collection was built up in Paris and London; he knew most of the emigré artists, most notably Benois and Bakst, and his bequest of some 68 items to the Ashmolean (1949) laid the foundation of its remarkable collection of Russian stage and costume designs. A replica of this drawing is in the Russian Museum, Leningrad.

▼115 John Nash (1893–1977): *Gloucestershire landscape*, canvas, 50 × 60 cm. The Nash brothers, John and Paul, were both prominent in the development of English painting between the wars. Paul (well represented in the Museum by drawings and prints) became a major force in English surrealism. John's most original and effective phase, of which our painting of 1914 is an early and quietly beautiful example, achieved a remarkable balance between a formal simplification abstracted from landscape and the retention of a strong and lyrical feeling of the physical reality of his subject matter, Gloucestershire fields and trees and hills. Given by the New Grafton Gallery and the Trustees of the John Nash Estate, 1978.

►116 Stanley Spencer (1891–1959): *Cows at Cookham*, canvas, 76.2 × 50.8 cm. Spencer was a highly individual artist, in the English mystical tradition of Blake. The simplifications and exaggerations of form here owe something to the formal explorations of painters in France following Cézanne (and to early Italians like Giotto), but his vision remained intensely, even eccentrically, personal. He divined – and painted – the lineaments of paradise in the modest, red-brick, rural village where he was born, Cookham on the Thames. This sheer celebration, of spring merging into summer, of the irrepressible vitality of human, beast and nature, is undisturbed by the sinister and surreal intrusions that perplex many of his paintings. It was developed from an original tiny illustration for the month of May for an Almanac, 1926, and painted only in 1936. Bequeathed by Thomas Balston through the National Art-Collections Fund, 1968.

Since the publication of the first edition, the Ashmolean has been very fortunate in being able to add to the collections a number of important objects through gift, bequest or purchase. A small selection is included here. Apart from our gratitude to the continued generosity of private donors and the usual grant giving bodies, we would like to acknowledge the benefits to the Museum of the Government's recently instituted acceptance-in-lieu procedure.

The existing text of the volume remains unaltered.

Christopher White

◄117 Italian: *Ducat,* gold, 2.2 cm diameter (enlarged). Minted for Francesco Sforza, Duke of Milan (1450–66). Among the earliest portrait coinages of the Renaissance, it represents a ruler notable for having governed by virtue of his personal qualities rather than solely by constitutional right. The design of the coin is sometimes attributed to Cristofano Caradosso, although this appears doubtful since Caradosso's undoubted medal of Francesco Sforza was certainly made long after Francesco's death. The medallist Gianfrancesco Enzola is perhaps more likely to have been responsible, but the question remains open. Bequeathed by Owen Parsons, 1986.

◄**118** Egyptian: *Statuette of the God Ptah*, bronze, height 19 cm, Late Period. The statuette is a rare type of coloured bronze, inlaid with gold, for example in the black bracelets, and silver in the eyes. It is a masterpiece of miniature sculpture and undoubtedly the finest Egyptian bronze in the collection. It belongs to that class of small bronze votive figures of divinities which are a noteable feature of the last phase of Pharaonic art, when the gods became more accessible to man. The god Ptah, often referred to as 'beautiful of face', was one of the major national divinities of Ancient Egypt, a creator god whose chief cult centre was at Memphis. Bequeathed by Miss M.R. Tomkinson, 1986.

▲ **119** Indian, northern Gujarat
or southern Rajasthan, post-
Gupta style, 9th century AD:
*Circular Ceiling Slab with eight armed
Men*, sandstone, diameter 76 cm.
Such slabs carved in high relief
were commonly used as ceiling
decoration in the temples of
western India and the Deccan.
Eight armed warriors, their
feet intertwined, radiate from a
centre like the spokes of a wheel;

each brandishes a sword. These
figures may represent *vidyadharas*
('bearers of knowledge'), magical
air beings who wield the sword of
knowledge which cuts through
ignorance. There are no other
identifying iconographic features
except for low-reliefs of flames on
the ground. Acquired 1985, with
a grant from the V&A Purchase
Grant Fund.

►**120** Roman: *Head of a Roman
Emperor*, porphyry, 21.5 cm, 4th
century AD. This fragmentary
head of a diademed figure almost
certainly comes from a late
Roman imperial relief, although
the face, which appears to have
been severely pock-marked, has
been smoothed and polished in
post-antique times. It possibly
represents the emperor Gratian
(359–83), aged about nineteen
or twenty, and may have been
broken off from a larger group of
paired tetrarchs. It represents a
beautiful example of porphyry
sculpture, of which authentic
examples are rare. Acquired 1994.

▼ **121** Spanish, probably Cordova (dated AD 999): *Carved Box Lid*, ivory, 10.5 cm. Carved from an elephant's tusk, this beautiful lid is decorated with the figures of four huntsmen killing deer and leopards. Most unusually, it is dated and inscribed with the name of the patron, the vizier Abu'l-Mutarrif. He was one of the last members of the Umayyad dynasty, whose fall saw the beginning of the Christian reconquest. Originally part of a casket, the lid almost certainly was made in Cordova, one of the two main centres of ivory carving in Muslim Spain. It is outstanding both for the representation of movement and for the quality of the detail. Acquired 1987, with grants from the V&A Purchase Grant Fund, the National Art Collections Fund and the Friends of the Ashmolean.

▲ **122** Nicola da Urbino (active 1520–1537/8): *Plate with women gathering flowers,* maiolica, diameter 30.5 cm, *c.*1525. This dish shows a group of women in an idyllic landscape, apparently disturbed by the arrival of a messenger bringing news; the exact subject, possibly from classical myth or literature, remains obscure. The dish is a characteristic work of Nicola at the height of his powers, produced about the time he painted the celebrated set for Isabella d'Este, Marchioness of Mantua, and illustrates, in the band surrounding the central image, the technique known as *bianco sopra bianco,* in which a design in opaque white is painted onto an off-white glaze. Acquired 1993, with grants from the MGC/ V&A Purchase Grant Fund, the National Art Collections Fund and the Friends of the Ashmolean.

►**123** Giovanni Bellini (active from *c*.1459; d. 1516): *Virgin and Child*, panel, 32.5 × 27.2 cm, *c*.1460–5. This touching and intimate portrayal of the Virgin and Child must be among the earliest of Bellini's works. (The gold background is clearly modern and probably replaces a discoloured area of sky or drapery). The sculptural quality of the figures reflects the influence of his elder brother-in-law, Andrea Mantegna. The apparent missing finger on the Child's right hand is probably an example of the young artist's mannerism of joining the central figures together. Bequeathed by Lord Clark of Saltwood and the bequest renounced so that the painting could be accepted by HM Government in lieu of inheritance tax and allocated to the Ashmolean Museum, 1987.

►**124** Peter Paul Rubens (1577–1640): *Thomas Howard, 2nd Earl of Arundel (1585–1646),* pen and brush in brown ink over black and red chalk, with washes of white bodycolour, 28 × 19 cm. Probably made from the life by Rubens when he was in England in 1629/30, the drawing was almost certainly taken back to Antwerp to serve as a record of the Earl's likeness, although it does not correspond exactly with any of three known paintings. In superb condition, and in an unusual combination of media, it is one of the finest portrait drawings by the artist in existence. Acquired 1994, with grants from the National Heritage Memorial Fund, the National Art Collections Fund, the MGC/V&A Purchase Grant Fund, the Michael Marks Charitable Trust and the Friends of the Ashmolean.

Index

(Numbers refer to illustrations unless otherwise indicated)